Yellow Cab

YELLOW CAB

Robert Leonard

University of New Mexico Press

Albuquerque

Library of Congress Cataloging–in–Publication Data

Leonard, Robert, 1954–
Yellow cab / Robert Leonard.
    p. cm.
Includes bibliographical references and index.
ISBN-13: 978-0-8263-3785-6 (pbk. : alk. paper)
ISBN-10: 0-8263-3785-6 (pbk. : alk. paper)
1. Albuquerque (N.M.)—Literary collections.
2. Taxicab drivers—Literary collections. I. Title.
PS3612.E574Y45 2006
                    2005023818

Design and composition: Mina Yamashita

Contents

YELLOW CAB

Dead Man's Curve

A wave of her threadlike hand caught my eye. Barely. My mind processed the flickering image and the hand grew large, separated, and turned into a pair of human silhouettes perched on the curb out front of the Hotel Blue. They were a pair of flags hoping for a ride out of downtown Albuquerque. The street was glistening wet after a passing thunderhead, but the summer storm had gone east. My eyes squinted against the sun, but not for long, as it was quickly sinking amidst pink and purple clouds and contrails behind Los Volcanoes. I turned my big worn steering wheel toward the figures and the rest of my cab followed reluctantly. I popped the meter on with my thumb even before I glided to a stop before them in my yellow Crown Vic. She reached the cab door first, thought about touching it, but didn't, waiting for him. I relaxed. If I had a gun like most drivers I might have relaxed my grip on its pearl, aluminum, or wood handle. But I didn't. Both she and I watched him open the door for her—approvingly. They climbed into the back of my cab, and I smelled sour booze. My hackles contemplated raising, but thought better of it. At least it isn't the sweet smell of crack, I thought. And it's a girl and a guy. Safe enough. I relaxed one more time.

"Thank God you stopped!" she said, scuttling across the bench seat to the far door to give him room.

"No problem. Glad to help," I replied cheerfully, thinking tip.

I had only caught a glimpse of them when their silhouettes had turned human and before they settled in as bodiless voices behind me. She was a sweet-faced, Navajo girl, long legs, flat butt, dressed in denim jeans and a jean jacket. White blouse and boots. Long, perfect, black hair, tugged taut and straight as if by some magical force. Some old boyfriend's inlaid string tie. Zuni, I thought. No, Navajo doing Zuni. Too bad about the flat butt, I thought. A little punctuation and she would be as perfect as her hair, but drunk.

"Yes," he grunted, air rushing out of his lungs as he bent over and in, his *panza* forcing it out of his chest. He settled in solidly beside her, behind me. The car leaned his and my way. "Thank you very much," he added.

He's not from here, I thought, listening to him. From back east somewhere. Shithead.

I bled the gas pedal. The cab rocked and eased into traffic.

"You folks going anywhere in particular?" I asked politely, thinking tip yet again. I always thought tip.

I could feel his body turn to look at her. Drivers don't see what's happening in their backseats. We feel it.

"Dead Man's Curve," she said laughingly, touching my shoulder lightly. "Do you know where Dead Man's Curve is?"

"Sure," I said, pleased I was going the wrong direction. I put on the turn signal, pulled a grand, wide U'ey on west Central, and pointed my yellow behemoth east effortlessly. Right on Eighth Street, south to Bridge, east to Isleta, then south, I planned. Dead Man's Curve, where Isleta swerved, no—bolted, forty-five degrees to the right before heading gently south again.

I felt her weight shift in the back of the cab. She was moving closer to him. The dispatcher's voice on the radio squawked, and I turned the radio down, but not too much. There might be another fare going my way.

I heard her sigh contentedly, with a warm giggle tacked to the end. Her voice wound up six inches lower than it had been. A flash of his hand in my rearview mirror let me know she was snuggling in, and he was placing his arm around her. Arching my back a little, in the rearview mirror I could see the top of her head, framed by his shoulder and right hand.

"Can you tell that we are in love?" she asked me. I felt her eyes on him. I ignored a yellow light and pressed through it.

"Knew it the moment I saw you," I replied without hesitation, still thinking tip.

"Can you tell HOW much we are in love?" I punched the button for an extra passenger. It allowed me to charge an extra fifty cents. I nodded at the same time, knowing she could see my head nod, even if I couldn't see her. I smiled and turned my head slightly to the right so she could catch a glimpse of the corner of my mouth and my smile. Now I can make some money, I thought. I kept my eyes on the road. Now heading south, I saw a mere sliver of a moon beginning to rise to the southeast over the Manzanos. The damn daylight was nearly gone. Sun always in your eyes and too hot to be comfortable with a half-ass cab air conditioner.

"It's our anniversary," she said. "We've been together one year now, haven't we dear?"

He paused for a moment before answering. "Why, yes my sweet. We have. We have indeed." He chuckled.

"We met in Paris," she said. "At a small café. I could only afford a pastry, coffee, and water, and was thinking about my lover—my ex-lover, I should say—when this lovely man seated next to me asked why my eye held a tear. I told him, and we have been together ever since!" She put her arms around him and squeezed. He sighed. "Do you know why I love him so?"

"Because he treats you like you should be treated, and not all men have treated you that way," I said.

"Why yes," she said. "How did you know?"

I thought about telling her the truth—that everyone who had ever warmed the seat she sat on had relationships with others who didn't treat them well—but instead I shrugged and lied, saying instead, "I could see how much he loved you in his eyes when you flagged me down." This didn't answer her question but it didn't matter.

I felt the warmth of her smile on the back of my neck. "Did you know he is a member of the Gould family, the Goulds of New York?"

"Nope," I said, thinking about his accent.

"That would be the railroad Goulds," she said. "Pioneers, magnates, philanthropists. They built libraries, saved the lives of poor orphans, and built the railroads that brought settlers west."

And brought the people that tried to drive your tribe into oblivion, I thought but didn't say.

He tapped me on the shoulder. My shoulder jerked slightly and involuntarily. She could touch me. He couldn't. But I took a deep breath and let it go. Maybe he recognized his error, maybe not. A moment passed.

"Excuse me sir," he said finally. "How much will the fare be—to this, this, uh, what is it? Dead Man's Curve?"

Cheap too, I thought. Don't get in a cab if you have to worry about the price of the fare.

"About fifteen bucks," I said. It was actually going to be closer to eleven, but if you estimate low and go over, a fare is pissed. Come in under, they are happy, and you might make the estimate up in tip. A high estimate always works for you one way or another.

"Don't you love that about rich people?" she said, laughing. "That is how they become rich—worrying about a buck or two here and there while you and I go off and spend every nickel as soon as it comes in. You and I do that, don't we, Mr. Driver?"

"Tell me about it," I said, only because I knew she wanted me to agree.

"Don't worry about the fare, sweetie," she said to me. "Richard has plenty of money, don't you dear?"

"Sure," said Richard, hesitantly. "Drive on, sir . . ."

"And Driver, honey, did you know that I am one of the famed Window Rock Begays?"

I laughed, then she did. Loudly. Window Rock is the capital of the Navajo Nation. The name Begay in Window Rock is like Smith in Washington, D.C.

"What's so funny?" Richard asked, ignorant but curious. I marked one up for him. Unlike most of the New Yorkers who have ridden in my cab, at least he didn't act like he knew everything when he didn't know anything. He's been here about a week, I thought, or he would know the significance of the name Begay.

"Never mind, dear. . . . I'll explain it to you later." She reached up and squeezed my shoulder twice, then patted it a few times platonically before drawing her hand back.

I could feel him nodding behind me, subserviently.

Suddenly, Dead Man's Curve loomed in front of me. My big foot slammed the brake pedal. It felt like mush, but caught in plenty of time to look like I planned it that way. The highway railing grew close and warning signs pointed for me to turn to the right.

"Turn left," she said, so I did. A hard left under the streetlight. Dead Man's Curve had only one streetlight above it. It was the only one in the neighborhood. Of course it was. Albuquerque didn't invest in this part of town. Poor people lived here— Hispanics, Indians, Mexicans, and white trash. They tended not to vote, and had better things to do with their nickels than buy lousy city councilmen.

I cruised slowly down Armijo Street until it turned into dirt. Waiting for instructions, I drove another fifty feet into the blackness.

"Stop here," she said. It was nowhere. The moon lit up the cornfields that surrounded us, and the closest house light was five hundred feet away. "Sorry, but I don't like anyone to know where I live. Nothing personal." I slowed to a stop and the dust we had stirred up in the road passed overhead to the east.

I felt her hand on my shoulder, and her cheek on mine, like a baby's eyelashes, for only a moment. I wished I had shaved.

Before the cab had stopped rocking, before the dust had settled, she was out of the taxi and in my headlights, on the dirt road that ran into what appeared to be a meadow. She raised her arms and began to dance in the headlights, turning gracefully, and slowly moving away, across my broad beams, into the night. She sang a lovely and haunting song I had never heard before.

"That'll be ten-fifty," I said to the man—Richard—still with me in the dark cab. Neither he nor I took our eyes off her. Her voice was enchanting. Lucky man, I thought.

Finally, I heard his door open. "OK," he said, getting out of the cab and lighting a cigarette. I rolled down my window and turned on the dome light so I could see what he was passing over. He opened his wallet and pulled out a ten and five ones and handed them to me, hesitantly.

"I don't know about this," he said, watching her pass through the margins of my headlights, slowly moving away from us. He blew cigarette smoke after her. I counted the money.

"What's not to know?" I asked, sliding the bills into my money roll. "It's your anniversary—she's a beautiful woman— she loves you—have fun."

"But it's not our anniversary," he said.

"So what?" I said impatiently, wanting to move on to my next fare. "Think of Paris, your future, your past, whatever makes her happy and have a good time. I gotta go." I put my car in reverse, hoping he would back away. He didn't.

"But you don't understand," he said, sounding worried, his hand on my door.

I quit thinking about my next fare and put the car back into Park. "What don't I understand?"

"We met for the first time tonight, in the bar at the La Posada, not a half-hour before you picked us up," he said, sadly.

"It's not your anniversary?" I said, noticing just how dark and isolated we were from the street.

"No!"

"You didn't meet in Paris?" I asked. I still heard her singing, and several dogs started barking. One howled.

"No!"

"Well, then don't go with her," I said, suddenly nervous. "This can be a tough part of town."

I thought for a moment. "Get in," I said. " I don't care if you don't have any money. I'll take you back to the hotel. You're not from here and could get hurt. Climb in and let's go."

He thought for a moment, but never took his eyes off the place where we had last seen her pass. He sighed, then straightened up, no longer leaning on the cab door. "No, I'll go with her," he said, slowly.

"Don't take the risk," I said. "You could get robbed, beaten up, or worse."

"Perhaps," he replied. "But there is something else you don't understand."

"What is that?" I asked.

"That I really have very little to lose."

With that, he folded his wallet, put it into his hip pocket, and passed into my headlights, following her. He stumbled across a rut, as if he had never been on a dirt road before, and then passed from sight into the night.

I waited for a few minutes, listening to the radio squawk, not caring that I missed a couple of good calls. Finally, I popped her into reverse, rolled her away from the ditch, and pointed west until the dirt road turned into pavement and Armijo into Isleta.

Turning right, I pushed her north, glancing back and forth between the road ahead and my rearview mirror. Dead Man's Curve grew smaller and smaller until the lone streetlight above it blinked out. 🔲

Albuquerque Sunport on an April Evening

At the port
fares gushed by us like schools of fish
skirting a coral reef rather than our taxi cabs,
when the image came of the water-hauling gray-haired
cabby from Poland with his white T-shirt and blue jean shorts
past his knees and south of his Poppin' Fresh bulge of a tummy
that I hadn't seen in awhile.

And so I turned to the driver of the cab behind me
and asked big pipe-smokin' Bob, "Hey, what happened to Polish?"

Jeannette, the pregnant, morning-sick, blond security guard
blew her whistle at a speeder, just one of dozens pouring
down the tunnel past us, intersecting the wave of fares
to take them home when they should have been riding with us.

"He died," Bob said, pulling his pipe from his mouth.
"His brother flew in from Poland and found him on the floor
of his apartment bled to death internally with a bottle
of some fancy Russian vodka in his hand."

Bob got a shitty 5 dollar off and back to the Airport Comfort Inn
and I got a 250 dollar bill to drift my yellow Crown Vic
through the New Mexican desert and stars east to Clovis
wondering what kind of a ride Polish got. ▨

Twice a Year

Twice a year, like clockwork,
As predictable as the migrations
of doves.
New college girls take to the streets.
Round faced and lovely
they sparkle
and tempt
to the bone.

School's out,
and in May money is needed
for the summer's journey home

And in December,
there are holiday presents
to buy,

for those they love. ▦

High Hopes

I followed the dusty, smoking Greyhound bus into the station like a hopeful old dog nudging its master hoping for a bone. Give them a little time to unload their luggage, and I might have a fare, I thought. To reach the taxi stand I pulled in front of the unattractive low building that represented the very worst of 1960s transportation architecture. As I came to a stop, for safety's sake I sorted the bits of humanity that buzzed around the front of the depot like flies around a trash can. Three bums hanging out across the street. Drug dealer on the corner. A wide-eyed teenage girl bumming money from a couple of travelers laying over who didn't have the sense to stay inside. I recognized no immediate threats, so I pulled my newspaper off the dashboard and opened it. Security must agree, I thought, noticing that there were no officers in sight as I penciled in a three-letter word for table scrap into the crossword puzzle. Ort.

The flash of a reflection off the opening bus-station door caught my eye. Out walked a middle-aged black man. Slender, five feet eight or so, blue-and-white plaid short-sleeve shirt, khakis, loafers. The clothes not only make the man, but they make the fare. Definitely safe, I thought. I saw him stumble, then catch himself. He looked at me, a bit embarrassed, and I knew I had a fare.

His movements were odd. At first I thought he might have been drinking, but his movements were a bit too stiff—too halting for a drunk, not sloppy. I might not have noticed his movements had they not been accentuated by his luggage, a blue Wal-Mart happy-face plastic bag that bounced way too much with each step he took. For reasons I am unsure of, I got out of my cab and walked around to the curb to meet him. He smiled and I nodded. He stepped off the curb and fell, face first, into the side of the cab. He bounced off, and I caught him. He was lighter than I had imagined and I caught a whiff of an odd metallic smell.

"Sorry about that," he said, as I helped him into the cab. He didn't seem to be able to bend very well.

"No problem," I replied, wondering what the hell had just happened as I climbed behind the wheel and launched the cab north and away from the curb.

"Where to?" I asked.

"The Sahara Motel, please. I understand it is close to the VA Hospital."

"That it is," I said, quite pleased, thinking of the eighteen or twenty bucks I would make on the run.

I slipped through the movie theater traffic and pulled between a couple of low riders and headed east on Central toward the freeway. Changing lanes, I nailed two green lights and would have caught them all the way to I-25 if it hadn't been for some asshole in front of me who was driving the speed limit.

"Long trip?" I asked.

"Not bad," he replied. "Just from Alamogordo. I live there."

Lovely and historic Alamogordo, nestled among the beautiful peaks of the Sacramento, Andres, and Organ mountains. Nearby were the spectacular dunes of the White Sands National Monument. Not so lovely were the dunes blown to hell and beyond by the militaries of a dozen nations at White Sands Missile Range. And then there is the nearby Trinity site, the location of the world's first nuclear bomb blast. The town motto could well be *Alamogordo—smack dab 'tween Heaven and Hell.*

"You like Alamogordo?"

"It's friendly. I was stationed there after the war—Vietnam— and I guess it kind of grew on me."

The light changed and I pulled onto the freeway. The metallic smell had reappeared. It soon filled the cab. It was pungent and acrid, like sour steel wool caught at the back of your throat. I realized that it was coming from my passenger. I contemplated asking him if it was his breath, or the product of some substance that oozed from his pores. Instead I coughed, rolled down the window, and drove faster.

The meter read $18.20 when I pulled up in front of the painted palm trees beside the lobby doors of the Sahara Motel. I climbed out of the cab and went around to open his door. I held it open, and he grabbed the door handle with his left hand and the side of the cab with his right. After a couple of tries, he managed to jerk himself out of the seat and onto his feet. I shut the door and he rested against the side of the cab as he fought his wallet out of his pocket. Finally he opened it, and his fingers shook and flicked at the bills inside, but didn't catch any.

"Would you mind taking a twenty and a one out?" he asked.

"Be happy to," I said, taking out the money, making sure that he could see everything I was doing with his wallet before I handed it back to him. I folded and stuffed the twenty and the one together into my shirt pocket.

"They sprayed a lot of shit on us in Vietnam, you know. And not just Agent Orange," he said.

"I read about that," I replied, now realizing the source of his problems. "So you come here regularly for treatment?"

"No," he said, "I've never been here before." He used his arm to push away from the cab and caught his balance with a few choppy steps. I raised my arms and took a step in case I had to catch him, but didn't have to.

"But," he continued, "I'm here to see the VA doctors. I think that maybe I have some sort of neurological problem." He paused, looking at me for a response.

"Could be," I said. "Could be." ▣

Manny

Big ol' Manny
all 6 feet 6 inches of him,
all 350 plus pounds of him,
a giant man-plum,
who packs his body into
his cab like a
pimento stuffed
into an olive,
says over the radio
to Butch the dispatcher,

**Woah, that was one fine
big mama just got outta my cab.**

And Butch says back,
you like 'em big Manny?

**You kiddin'? I'm a big man—
a ravenous man
a man with voracious appetites
in all things.
Skinny Halle Berry looks
like a dyin' crack whore
to me.
Give me a big woman
a pear-shaped woman
with whoppin' thighs,
thighs I can sink my teeth into.
Juicy.**

Ooo yeah. ▦

Stardust

A glistening, white grub-worm
climbed into my cab at the Stardust Hotel,
and we coasted downhill—westbound—on Central, Route 66
piercing the surreal neon, glass, and gummy asphalt, and lunging
under the railroad tracks, only to
POP out on the other side, bouncing, drifting toward the
     Launchpad bar.

The grubworm, segmented, pale, and unshaven,
wore dusty Levis, a black Metallica T-shirt, a
John Deere cap, and a drunk's sagging face and dying eyes.
"I wanna be a good man some day," he said.
"But I'm not now."
"Good luck," I said.

"Luck?" he snorted and spit.
"Luck? You think luck is what it takes, you ignorant bastard?"
"What does it take then," I said.
"Nothin,'" he said. "Nothin' you or I can do.
The TRUTH is, God either loves you, and you prosper,
Or he hates you, and you suffer and then he sends you
     straight to hell."

And he paused, and said,

"And he hates most of us. Including you,
And me,
And especially me."

White Boy

To my right D.J. sat slumped in the seat of his cab, blue baseball cap peeking out over the open hole of the driver's window. Troy's cab was pulled up to my left, and from my driver's seat I heard the robotic, metallic clacking of two weapons being checked. In stereo. D.J. was a downtown rat like me, but we were in holding, hoping for the airport to pop. Nothing was happening yet, and if it didn't soon, it was likely that D.J. would exit the night and go home and play video games till it was dawn and time to turn in the cab. Troy avoided downtown whenever possible, preferring the heights, and hopefully, long runs out of Sandia Casino.

The radio cackled, and Jerry the dispatcher gave a call to a driver logged downtown. "243 . . . Allsup's Fourth and Bellamah."

"Hate those fuckin' Fourth and Bellamah calls," said Troy, rubbing his shaved and polished head.

"Me too," said D.J. "One time I was assaulted with a burrito there."

"How the hell you get assaulted with a burrito?" asked Troy.

D.J. sat up in his seat, adjusting his ponytail. "Well, I picked up this cholo-looking bastard, wife-beater T-shirt, tattoos all the way up his neck, climbing up to his face, pants half down around his ass, hairnet, regular low-life gangbanger. He climbs in munching a fuckin' Allsup's burrito, drippin' green chile all over the place, and I said 'no food in the cab,' and 'I'm gonna need some money up front.' Simple as that. And then he pops out this switchblade, pokes it at me, and says, '*jeest* drive, *white boy*, and shut *da* fuck up before I *fuckeeng steek* you.' And the next thing I know without even thinking I have this in his face and he's looking at me all cross-eyed."

D.J. holds up his .38 Special and shakes it a couple of times.

"And then I said, 'do you want me to drive before or after I blow your brains out all over the backseat, you *pinche cabron* . . .'" And so he gets out of my cab and throws the burrito at me and it hits the fender and I drive back to the shop and wash it off."

"Did you get his knife?" asked Troy, his black slits for eyes narrowing.

"No, didn't even think about it, it happened all so fast."

"Oh, ya gotta get the knife," said Troy. "I always get the knife." ▣

26 seconds

Digital clocks tick, tick, tick,
next to the white icons
of men walking at
all the new crossing lights
near the university.

26, 25, 24,
and on, till the orange hand
pops up, blinking, saying
hurry, or stop—but be sure
to make up your mind.

8, 7, 6,
seconds become a challenge
to a sprint, certainly not the
intention
of the designer.

And sprint they do,
some glide like pigeons,
others with trouser legs
filled with sand.

3, 2, 1,
I love the look on the
professors' faces, when their young minds,
having forgotten their creaky, spindly legs,
see me

accelerate.

El Abuelo de Jesús

Cops circled the crowd like a pack of hungry coyotes around clustered sheep. Police cruisers blocked Central at Third, Fifth, and at the T where Fourth Street terminated at Central, choking the partying crowd as they spilled out of a half-dozen downtown bars. It was at closing time. The crowd, mostly college age, didn't seem to notice the police as they laughed, hugged, flirted, and said their drunken farewells. I slipped my cab between a couple of cruisers and a Street Closed sign and next to Jesús, who had parked his cab at a spot where he could be easily seen by the crowd. Cabdrivers are largely ignored by the cops at this time and place, enjoying a fragile protected status against breaking traffic laws. Occasionally a rookie hassles us until a vet lets him in on a secret—when people are drunk, cabdrivers save lives.

Jesús leaned against his cab, his long thin body draped like a rope across the top of his open car door. Jesús always wore exactly the same thing—a dark blue T-shirt, Levi's, and black combat boots. This man with the raven ponytail was a lifeboat for some of these people, only they were too caught up in closing time to know it yet. A rumor has it that Jesús was once homeless, but found out that cabdrivers led an easier yet equally unstructured life. He walked over to my cab.

His long fingers gestured toward the activity on the street. "If I was in there and saw the look on those lousy cop faces I would run like hell," he said. "Those cops, they are looking to kick the shit out of someone and if I was in there you know it would probably be me they would be looking to kick."

I got out of my cab and leaned against it, watching the crowd for anyone with that "I want a ride really bad" look in their eyes, while Jesús kept talking.

"Let me tell you a secret," he said, tossing his ponytail over his shoulder. "*Mi abuelo* said to me all the time when I was a kid; 'kid,' he would say, 'it is better to run like a chicken than to be like a tough-ass rooster lying in the dirt dead with a bunch of cops or other *pendejos* beatin' you with sticks or clubs or something or shooting you in your brain or kicking you in the *huevos*.'

"And for that partying, not me man, *mi abuelo* he said to me once when I was about fourteen and starting to hang out with a party crowd and drinkin' and doing a bit of weed, you know, he said to me, '*míjo*, hey, you like to party, well every man has to party and that's OK, and hey, you know little Ruben Valencia, hey he liked to party once too, and he had hisself a good job there at the mall, could buy all the beer he wanted, all the girls liked him, and hey he even bought hisself a new Firebird, all red and clean, well, not really new but only about three years old or so, and hey, Ruben he met these guys over there by the river, and they all went together into the *bosque* and were drinking and partying and havin' fun and lookin' at the stars and comets and shit and doin' some weed and next thing old Ruben knew was that he woke up in the mornin' with an achin' head, naked on the hood of his Firebird, and his ass hurt.'

"And I been careful partying ever since."

His eyes darted away from mine, and I looked too. The cops were starting to close in on the crowd. Several were fingering their nightsticks, and a young lady cop was pulling out a bullhorn.

Jesús cupped his hands around his mouth, and tossed back his head.

"Hey!" he shouted to the crowd. "Time to go home! This way! Taxi, Taxi!

"RUN LIKE CHICKENS!" 🔳

Entrepreneurs

I lean on my cab while a businessman
from the Hyatt suffers uneasily in the 6:00 p.m. line of men
at Stadium Liquors. His health-club-toned body,
fresh and crisp in an Armani suit and Gucci loafers,
stands out amidst the work-hardened,
thickly veined, unshaven men in dirty tar- or paint-stained *ropas*
and *zapatas* from thrift stores or the Kmart on Atrisco.

A clown circles the trash-strewn asphalt lot, pushing a dusty white cart
that says *Paletas* in lime-green letters. Low riders and pickups
cruise through,
as children smile or stare fascinated at the clown, circling.
The clown wears the same baggy Wranglers and white T-shirt
as the rest of the men from Barelas who trickle out,
carrying twelve-packs and paper sacks wrinkled around the necks of
    mystery bottles.
But his shoes are several sizes too big, and he wears a faded plastic
    red nose and a floppy hat,
and a different kind of weariness than the rest of the men, as he circles.
His bright yellow beach umbrella shades the ice cream from the
    afternoon sun
a little, but the radiant heat from the asphalt is his real foe.
From the yellow umbrella dangle plastic blow-up green Hulks,
Powerpuff Girls, and one brown deflated Pooh.

"Take me to a liquor store and back," the businessman had said,
climbing in, pleasantly streaming words at me, including returns
    on investments,

stock options, diversification, economic stimulation, and why tax cuts
   are good
for everyone including you and me because it all trickles down
and as everyone knows, a rising tide raises all boats,
and all of this before the stop light at Tijeras and Third Street,
and so I took him to a liquor store, not the closest, or the best, but to
   Stadium Liquors in the
barrio where I knew a round trip would get me a twenty-five-dollar bill
   or so.
The businessman smiles when he trots out of the store,
gleeful in escaping the pressure of the presence of men different
   from him,
his bottle of Blue Sapphire, sans bag, hugged closely to his chest
and when he nears, I point—and say,

buy something from the clown,

and the man pauses and doesn't know what
to do and so I say, more gently—

it's our custom to buy something from the clown.

And then,

Trickle down to the clown, I say
Trickle down to the clown.
Raise his boat!

And so he moves to the clown, and the clown graciously
points out his wares to the man in Spanish, which he doesn't
   understand,

and so I say,

Buy a Hulk,
Or a Powerpuff Girl,
or maybe Pooh,
at least an ice cream!

And so he buys an ice cream,
and it goes drip, drip, drip
on the floor of my taxi,
all the way back to the Hyatt.

Dining Out

Most of the time the tourists
in their relaxed-fit name brands
are an enthusiastic, happy crowd,
very egalitarian in their treatment
of drivers and curious to obtain
all sorts of sensory experiences that
young bellboys and hotel counter girls
are largely ignorant
of.

And so they ask us worldly cabdrivers
their questions regarding the best
satiation destinations, which mainly
revolve around fine dining, preferably
with a view, and in a beautiful setting
perhaps adobe, with vigas, and candles
or a lively patio with Calliope hummingbirds
wandering from flower to flower
and mariachis from table to table.

Or maybe just a beautiful man dressed
in black playing guitar like Ottmar Leibert—
who cares, as long as all five senses are
filled to bursting, the flavor of the meal,
its aroma, the flickering flames against earthen
walls and stone floors and the music to say
nothing of fine dinner conversation and the cool
sweaty touch of sweaty crystal wine glasses filled with
red maybe the only way they could add to their

pleasure would be if an anonymous and lovely
someone were to diddle them under the tablecloth
most discreetly.

And we try to answer the questions the best we can,
and take them to only the very best destinations they
seek, but some of the questions about cuisines that are
asked mainly to impress dinner companions riding
uncomfortably thigh to thigh in the backseat just might stump Emeril,
and while your average taxi driver knows that the "peppers"
at the airport Waffle House are really green *chiles,* and that
it is important to always order your *huevos rancheros* on a flour
tortilla when at Garcia's Kitchen, and that you have to ask for margarine
for your tortillas at the Frontier, *haute cuisine* isn't our bailiwick.

And so while an old driver or two might remember someplace they took
their ex-wives to eat on a fancy occasion when they were still wives
against their better judgment a lifetime ago, mostly we just run
on at the mouth and act like we know what we are talking about
and take them places we take everyone else who seems to know
a worthwhile destination to dine and the farther away the better,
and would you like my cell number to bring you back?

But then a new driver might not know better and call in and ask
Butch the dispatcher where a good place is for Italian, Greek,
    New Mexican,
or you name it food, and Butch always answers, in his own unique and
inimitably polite yet irritated way—

How the hell would I know? The only time I go out to eat
is when I take a peanut butter and jelly sandwich to the park.

City of Cats

Ghosts are everywhere—all the night drivers see them. Most of the time they appear in the dead time, that time spent fighting sleep, when the radio is so dead you begin to think that it never worked, and when you believe that you must be completely alone in the world. Occasionally they come in daylight when the taxi is rolling and dart past the corner of your eye, but most of the time they come out of the stillness of the night when you are parked in your favorite, safe place on the streets—that lovely, special spot where you know no one is going to fuck with you—and at the time when you are so tired that your eyes are open but you are not seeing this world but another one and the colors swirl from the street, seeping into your eyes and into your brain and you are so tired you can feel the capillaries in your face pop like microscopic fireworks. The ghosts trickle out in front of you, mockingly alive, with most of them taking form as they emerge from something else of more substance—escaping into the material world, slipping out of a streetlight, a cholla, or a dumpster only to slide into another piece of our world or another before your brain can really process that they were there. But it does and they were. With varying degrees of translucency, they oscillate in and out like the signal from a late-night radio station several states away, only to finally fade away as dawn breaks. In another place and time scholars may have called their corporeal bodies ether, or phlogiston, or maybe protoplasm. Yet these names would all have been wrong as in reality they have no more substance than the perfume of a pretty girl who passed several minutes ago. And sometimes they don't fade into something else but into near nothingness instead, and all that remains is the faintest hint of them, floating, just barely there, like the breath of a sleeping newborn on mama's breast.

Sometimes they are people you think you know, or more often pieces and concatenations of people and things that you know you know but can't remember. Sometimes they are as far away as the horizon; other times they startle you, emerging in the nexus of your lap and your coffee cup. One once formed for me out of the intersection of the blackness of the night sky and a cumulus cloud curled over the face of the Sandias, and another looked me in the eye from my dashboard before it was gone. Often the same one, a man I know but never met, rides in my backseat, and I only see him through the rearview—a pale, long dead, sixtyish cabdriver in a red plaid fishing cap.

But they are always there, and real, and the cats see them, and look at them with interest until they are gone and a bit longer. The city is full of cats, and they know who you are and what you are doing in the world even though you do not. They're just not telling. The cats are tabby and gray and black and orange and white and brown and spotted and striped and mottled or a million other colors and combinations of fur, and at night most of the time they are half a block away and moving at the same pace the ghosts move, only more solid. And they always watch you coming down the street, not because you drew their attention, but because they just knew you were coming and had known forever. Sometimes the cats race across the street in pursuit or in fear of the ghosts, I can't tell, other times they sit quietly unnoticed but then noticed; and the city is thick with them, so crammed with them you have no idea unless you are a night driver or a whore or the rare cop who actually pays attention to the world.

The whores see the cats, and the ghosts too. They love the cats because the cats come out of the night and purr and meow and rub up against them lovingly and the cats don't care if they are whores or the Queen of England. But the whores fear the ghosts because the ghosts come out of the night for them too and fuck them and don't pay and they remember these encounters the rest of their lives, whether they want to or not. And somehow I don't think that the Queen of England sees these ghosts like the whores do.

And the whores see us cabdrivers too, a continual string of little islands of yellow afloat in the river of the night, offering safe passage to any girl in trouble that cops and pimps can't or refuse to offer. They know we offer safe passage out of a bad situation when they need it and when you are a whore almost all situations are bad or are going to be soon, and we don't care if they don't have any money because we probably don't have anything more important or interesting to do than help a girl in trouble and besides they never want a ride very far and who would want to take trick money from a hard-working whore anyway?

And sometimes we night drivers are like the ghosts too, oozing around corners and popping into places where we may or may not be wanted, in a perpetual liminal state, dropping between one world and another, and for a variety of reasons people ride with us there—no one really wanting to be with us, but needing us to get from one of their worlds to another. We are ghosts in these fares' lives, moving them from one material world to another, boatmen on a contemporary River Styx or one of its tributaries. And the cats sit on the banks of our river, and they watch us intently, because it is, after all, their city. They were here before us, and will remain after our city lies in ruins. The cats, the rats, the cockroaches, and their kin will linger. Maybe a few whores too, as it is clear that God holds a special—if not good—place in his heart for the whores of the world. For, as the ancient parable goes, as sure as God hears the sparrow fall, he hears a working girl turn a trick.

As do the cats, the only difference being that they, unlike God, seem to care. ▦

7901 East Central

They stood on the curb in Barelas,
young lovers kissing under the streetlight,
touching fingers, then parting sadly,

she climbed into my cab smelling of
violets and soap.

He watched us drive away,
putting his cigarette out
on the lamppost
then turning.

Away.

"Isn't he handsome?" she asked,
and I said, *"Oh yes."*
"He's my husband."
"He's in a band."
"He loves me."

"I can tell," I said.

And I drove her to 7901 East Central,
past Pennsylvania, behind the Pussycat,
where frat boys and truckers will find her
amidst the other girls,

if she is lucky. ▧

Just Hang Up

The digital clock on the PNM building turned 3:15 a.m. when I saw Eduardo round the corner at the bus and drift in next to me where I was parked.

"How's your night going?" I asked as he put his cab into park.

He laughed from deep in his belly.

"Listen to this. I got that lottery in Los Lunas that came out about ten, and I called the guy and he seemed OK and so I went and didn't worry too much about it. I got turned around a time or two, but he led me in on the phone. Sure enough, he was coming to town. Downtown. A good run, you know. He was a middle-aged Hispanic dude dressed nice. Friendly, too.

"And so we get on the freeway northbound and I'm pushing it back hard and he gets on his cell and calls his wife, says something like 'cariña, I'm coming home tonight. I finished the work for your mom early, and I want to come back.'

"And she says something like she doesn't want him to go do all that work and come home, he must be tired and everything, and so he says, 'I know I was planning to stay overnight, but I'm done early and I'm sure you already put the kids to bed and I'll call out for some pizza and bring home some beer and we'll have some fun like we haven't in some time.'

"And I guess that she is all nice to him and everything, but she really doesn't want him to come home at all and he says that it's really not that late, and that he's not really that tired, even though he worked hard and all that but finally he gives in, and says that he isn't coming, says 'adios' and I think 'fuck, my sixty run looks like its gonna be a twenty instead if I have to go back to Los Lunas and I'm screwed and I hate fucking lotteries and I'm never going to take another again.' But he sits there after he says good-bye and doesn't say anything and the radio is quiet and then I hear something on his cell, even from the front seat. And I turn around and he has the cell in his hand and looks at it all puzzled like and then puts it at his ear.

"And he listens for awhile and then he puts the phone down and covers it and says to me, real sad and quiet like, that 'someone is fucking my wife.' His wife he means. And I say 'what?' And he says a little louder this time, and angrier, but not too loud— 'someone is fucking my wife—she must have forgot to hang up the phone and just set it on the dresser!' And I don't know what to say, and so I say 'you are shitting me' and he says 'no I'm not, believe me I'm sitting here in your damn yellow taxicab listening to someone fucking my wife.' So then he says 'listen' and hands me the phone and says 'does that sound like someone fucking my wife to you?' And so I take the phone and listen, and sure enough someone is fucking someone, and if that someone is his wife she is having a real nice time. And he says 'what does that sound like to you, and I say 'well, it sounds to me like someone is fucking your wife.'

"And he says 'drive faster,' and so I drive faster, and it's still not fast enough, but I don't want to go above ninety on the freeway and he understands that and doesn't get pissed, and then he starts sighing a bit and he is hurt and sad, and every once in a while he cusses but that's it. I would have been a lot more pissed, if it had been my wife and all, but he had more *cojones* than I do and he got all stoic-like. I remembered that I still had the cell to my ear, and so I quit listening to someone fucking his wife, because listening too long seemed like it must be rude or something even though he asked me to listen. But I don't want to give it back to him because he just shouldn't listen anymore. It's just not good, ya know, can you imagine? And then he says 'give me back my phone,' and I say 'you shouldn't listen,' and he says 'really, give me my phone I mean it,' and so I gave it to him and then he listens for just a minute or two, and then he says 'shit, listen to this,' and hands the phone back to me and I listen and believe it or not, all I hear is some guy moaning and groaning, and really enjoying himself and it must be this guy's wife doing him and I don't know what to say, but really the wife must be fucking this other guy's brains out his ears. And he says 'what does that sound like to you,' and I say 'it sounds like more fucking to me, just a different position,' and he says, 'that's what it sounds like to me too.' I was real careful not to mention the position I was imagining they were in because I didn't want to be an asshole or anything.

"And next thing I know we are off the freeway and he has me cruising up Broadway about sixty miles per hour, and I know we are close to his house and I get worried that he isn't going to mess around paying a taxi driver when he knows his wife is fucking some other guy, and so I see the meter is at fifty bucks, and tell him the fare is close enough to fifty if he wouldn't mind paying me now, and I didn't even know it, but the guy already has three twenties folded into his hand and he hands it to me and says 'keep it.' And next thing I know he says 'stop here, at that white house at the corner,' and so I stop, and he gets out of the cab, slams the door, and runs into this house. And I sit there a minute, but not too long since I don't have a reason just to sit there. And it's not like I could help or anything.

"And so, not knowing what else to do, I take a call, drive this other guy from the El Madrid bar to the west side. Another good run. But then I start wondering about the guy whose wife was fucking someone else, and since I have nothing better to do, I drive by his house again, and man there are cops everywhere. Everywhere. And an ambulance and a fire truck, and a bunch of neighbors standing around in pajamas and shit. But the cops wouldn't let me just sit there, and so I took another call. Maybe we will read what happened in the papers tomorrow, but I hope the guy is OK and that he kicked the shit out of the guy that was fucking his wife."

"And I hope she learns that next time she better just hang up the phone when she is fucking someone," I said.

"No shit," said Eduardo, laughing.

Crazies

Before I was a cabdriver,
I read about crazy people,
in the news,
from afar,
and I knew, surely knew,
that these exotic and fearsome creatures
were rare.

Now I listen to them rant and ramble,
from the backseat of my cab,
common as a March wind.
Some attain craziness through
the miracle of modern science,
or through potions of the ancients,
still others are artifacts of God.

And some may not be
crazy at all,
and I suspect that maybe
one or two
might have been
prophets instead.

If only I knew,
which ones.

A Gift from God

I was rolling west down Central, nearing Old Town, heading toward Garcia's Kitchen for a fare. The light on Tenth Street flashed yellow before I was close enough to the intersection to cruise through masquerading as a good citizen. In half an instant I decided I couldn't even fake it, so I hit the brake pedal, and the one brake working in the cab, the left rear, first tugged, then squealed, burning rubber when it realized it was all alone in the world. The car twisted to a stop halfway into the crosswalk.

I slumped in my seat, in cabdriver purgatory. There are few things worse for a cabdriver than sitting through a red light without a fare. We'd rather have a drunk asshole with money in the backseat than ride empty. With a fare, at least being stopped at the light gets us waiting time—twenty cents every thirty seconds.

And so there I sat, alone, at Tenth and Central.

Each second seems like ten for all of us whenever we are stuck at a light. We try to break the boredom, so we look around. It was early, still daylight, but at this light I had no ghosts to watch. I looked for anything moving, something to draw my interest. Driving down the same street thousands of times from the same angle offers little new to look at, so I employed an old trick I use—the full rotation head pivot. First, I turned my head ALL THE WAY to the right. Oh! there was a door in that building I had never seen before! I studied it for a moment. To complete the operation, I then turned my head ALL THE WAY to the left. Ah! A little tabby kitten under the stairs over there! I watched it chase its tail under the steps, then be startled by something I hadn't seen. It scuttled deeper under the stairs, shoulders hunched, back arched, fur at attention, and its tail flicking as its eyes followed movement across the street. My eyes followed the kitten's.

What caught the kitten's eye, and then mine, was a tall, thin Indian man at the edge of the crosswalk. Sky-blue T-shirt, Levis, black engineer boots, and a turquoise-and-silver rodeo belt buckle with a bucking bronc and rider on it. He had a handsome, square face, blunt nose, wide mouth above a few scattered chin whiskers. His shoulder length hair was streaked gray. He looked sixty-five, but might have been twenty years younger. His wrinkles had wrinkles, but his eyes sparkled. He rocked and bounced as he stepped off the curb and into the crosswalk. While he was elegant, his clothes weren't, and the Circle K plastic bag he was carrying with his clothes stuffed into it triggered a thought in my head—homeless.

And then I noticed that in the middle of the crosswalk, in his path, lay a cigarette butt. Actually, it was much more than a cigarette butt—it was actually half a cigarette. It was slowly burning, its smoke languidly rising in the still, early evening air. As his right foot hit the pavement, he spied the cigarette and paused briefly as if startled. Then, a slight smile crept upon his face. He approached the small pyre slowly, and with great gentleness, almost as if he was dealing with a sacred object, he stopped, bent over, picked up the cigarette, then, straightening, brought it tenderly to his lips. He closed his eyes and took a puff. A few seconds later, savoring every moment, he let the smoke find its own way out of his lungs, with only the slightest exhalation. He sighed deeply, his eyes opened, and he turned them toward the heavens. And there, in the crosswalk at Tenth and Central, he silently mouthed these tender words to someone or something above us all—thank you.

Meter Rate

Every couple of weeks or so,
a lady on Ridgecrest
calls for a cab,
and looking for some lovin',
answers the door in her
birthday suit.

She pays meter rate,
and tips well
for courteous and attentive
service.

Poor Danny B.,
a kind and gentle man,
who sells burritos his mom makes,
and Cokes out of the trunk of his cab,
hoped to get the call for months.

But when he did,
he brought roses and a smile,
and she cancelled him
at the door,
not liking something she saw,
through the
peephole. ▣

Un Poquito es Mejor que Nada

Hablo Español, un poquito—
I speak a little Spanish, I said,
under a slice of moon
to the man in the shadows,
hands folded, outside my cab.
Un poquito es mejor que nada—
a little is better than none, I thought
I heard him say, but maybe not,
near the blooming cholla that frames
the chain link gate of Americanos Busline,
where a bus idled,
shaking the ground like a vibrating bed with
a body-worn thin, brown, corded bedspread
I remember from a cheap motel where I stayed
in 1972, on my way to somewhere long forgotten,
as the bus spewed a familiar poison at me, and directly
into the bus driver's lungs as he unloaded bags,
killing him, but not yet.

A Cantinflas video from the '40s played
for the thousandth time
on eight screens simultaneously
to just one more load of passengers from El Paso,
Juárez, and points south, who stared mindlessly at
the mustachioed comedian as he pantomimed
terror, wanting so badly to take their swollen feet
and tired backs and minds off the bus but this wasn't

their stop and I saw an old Mexican lady point
and burst out laughing at Cantinflas or maybe me.
Traffic lights turned red and a void of cars appeared in
the street, and six weary men, dressed neatly, but not today,
clutched one small bag each and moved small from the shadows
across the sidewalk and filled all corners of my
cab, scraping doors, apologizing to each other,
and me, my cab sinking to the road, leaden with humanity.

The cab grew warm and humid and began to stink of men
as we drove northbound, to Santa Fe, at the speed limit
and using turn signals and every thing I could think of that
was legal except for one thing I was doing, and they gave me
money congratulating each other on their wisdom because
the seventy-eight dollar cab fare was 78/6=13 dollars each and
        cheaper than a
bus ticket and the fucking *migra* wasn't going to stop a taxi cab
like they would a bus, no?

And I worried if I was a *coyote*, a criminal and conveyor of illicit
human flesh who the officials of the United States of America
would put in prison, along with the men I hauled, who just like me,
        were only
thinking of wives, or girlfriends, and their children and the money
        they would soon be
able to send home, or was I just one more person doing one small
        thing on a modern
underground railroad 1848–2003 *porque un poquito es mejor
        que nada.* ▦

Crossroads Hotel

I picked her up at the Crossroads Hotel, across Central from Presbyterian Hospital. The Crossroads is a dump in the footprint of northbound I-25. The hotel is so precariously perched next to the Interstate that in an accident a car going over the rail might well catapult into an unsuspecting lodger's lap. She opened the door of the cab and the roar of traffic accompanied her and her nurse's flowered-print scrubs into my backseat. She stank of hospital, cheap whiskey, and more.

"Sorry, I just need to go to the Presbyterian parking lot and pick up my car," she said.

Shit, I thought. You could have hopped there on one leg faster than I can get you there, I wanted to say, but didn't.

"I know what you're thinking," she said. "You're thinking that I could have walked, but you know it isn't safe."

I nodded and turned onto Central to drive the couple of blocks to the parking lot, knowing she was right. That part of Central wasn't safe at all.

Something in her voice bothered me—it was impersonal and nearly robotic. At first I thought hers might be the standard, tired "nurse's voice" used for patients, but there seemed to be something else there as well.

"So," I said, "you live at the Crossroads because it's close to work?"

"Well, yes, temporarily I hope. Six months ago I left my husband and kids because I found the man of my dreams. He's tall, good-looking, wonderful, and has a good job with the city. I moved in with him, and now I'm three months pregnant."

"Congratulations, I guess," I said.

"Well, I don't know about that because three days ago the man of my dreams told me he doesn't really love me, never has, and that he has a new girlfriend who understands him in ways I don't. So he asked me to move out, and my husband says he doesn't want me back—at least not yet, and my parents haven't been very supportive, and Mom said that I made my own bed and must lie in it, and Dad said I'm an ungrateful slut, and they won't let me move in with them either, so I had to get a room at the Crossroads close to work."

I rolled through a stop sign and into the parking lot. She pointed to a battered old Toyota and I pulled up next to it.

"So, why do you think everyone is treating me so badly?" she said, handing me a five.

"I don't know," I said. "It's none of my business." And besides, I wanted to say—I've got work to do.

"Please? No one else will talk to me and I am so hurt and lonely."

"OK," I sighed, "here is how it is and it's not really very complex. They're pissed. You left your family for a man who just kicked you out. And they all have a right to be pissed. Nothing worked out and you screwed up your life. And theirs. Especially the kids. You fucked up and now you are stuck all alone in a shitty hotel on Central with the television and a bottle of whiskey for company and that's how it is. What more can I say?"

"That's not nice," she said.

"No, it isn't." Five in hand, I waited for her to get out of the car. She didn't. Instead she started crying.

"OK," I said, trying to be a bit more compassionate, "give

them some time. A few months. Maybe they will come around and support you. And if they don't come around and offer their support, with time maybe they will at least act like they do."

"Great," she said angrily. "That makes me feel better." She got out and slammed the door.

"And quit drinking," I said through the open window, raising my voice slightly. "It's bad for the baby."

"Fuck you," she yelled.

"That's highly unlikely," I replied, stepping on the gas and pulling away. 🔳

Brother

Robert Lowell,
the great American poet
born of wealth and station,
given everything
in life
that a man might need,
despised it nonetheless,
specifically because of
the privilege of it all.

Born at the wrong time,
a pacifist who protested
one of the few just wars
of the last century, the war
against Mussolini,
Tojo,
and Hitler.

Had a trainwreck of a life
three wives,
abandoned families,
dependencies that destroyed
a broken yet brilliant mind.

Robert Lowell, lithium eater,
straitjacket wearer.
Died of heart failure in
1977
in the back of a New York
City cab,
clutching a brown paper
parcel.

How sorry
I feel for my brother,
in whose cab,
Robert Lowell died.
With the meter still ticking,
for a dead man in the backseat. ▩

Judy

When Judy,
the bouncy hooker
who moonlights
at Emerald's,
where the sign says
"let your fantasies come true,"
calls your cell, asking for a ride,
you will know it's her when
she greets you with a hearty
"Ho, Ho, Ho."

Why We Are Here

About once a month,
when things are really bad
and there is no money to be had
out in the world,
Butch the dispatcher
makes it worse,
by telling us
cabdrivers

Remember,
we're all here,
'cause we're not
all there.

Better

The night sagged around me. Bar rush was over, and the small of the night—that time between hauling all the drunks home and taking fares to the airport for dawn flights—had arrived. A cold, winter rain had slicked the streets, and the neon movie marquee flickered above me at First and Central. I was alone, stopped at the red traffic light. I looked around, saw no one was coming in any direction, and would have run the red light if I actually had anywhere to go. Instead I sat there. After just a moment I felt life slip from my stare and my jaw droop, and it suddenly occurred to me that I might have sat through a green light in my favor. Or more. Nearly as suddenly I realized that a car had pulled up beside me. A young woman sitting behind the passenger seat of a shiny new Mitsubishi was leaning out of the passenger side window moving her right arm and hand in the universal Roll Down Your Window sign.

I dragged my left hand off my lap and managed to roll down my window. She was beautiful. So were the driver and the two young women in the backseat. Their half-smiles told me that something had amused them. I suspected that it was me.

"How are you tonight, sir?" she asked.

"I'm cold," I said.

She nodded sympathetically.

"I'm tired," I said.

She shook her head knowingly.

"I'm hungry," I said, and paused.

"Oh, I'm so sorry to hear that," she replied, smiling, and

nodding at the girls behind her. "Would this make you feel better?"

At that same moment, all four girls lifted their blouses and popped their breasts out from under their bras, and exposed eight perfect-nippled moons reflecting the neon marquee of the theater. Just as quickly the Mitsubishi then peeled out and the sound of laughter and the smell of exhaust enveloped me.

"Yeah," I said to myself, "that helps," as I sat through another green light. Or more. ▨

Walk

Sometimes,
when I sit at the red traffic light,
my eyes wander
to the left,
or the right,
to the little white crossing-walk man.
With one determined foot placed far ahead,
reaching, the other firmly planted, pushes off,
as if to drive his bent-over body
into some imagined wind.

One arm reaches forward, slightly bent
and I imagine his palm is turned upward,
following the lead of the purposeful foot,
the other arm, bent at the elbow,
behind his body, in
the ideal position
for powerful walking,
serving as an indication to the pedestrian,
to cross the street,
and to be sure to
do it
without dallying.

And I wonder,
why is the little white crossing-walk man
white?

Isn't it possible,
to have a little brown crossing-walk man,
or a red one, or a yellow one?
Or a black one, on say,
a field of white?

And then you must ask, Why not
even a green or blue or multicolored
little crossing-walk man,
and I'm sure that there is a computer in there
that could probably generate little crossing-walk men,
in random colors in the interest of fairness.

And why the indication to walk,
not to skip,
or hop,
or better yet,
dance across the street,
or even moonwalk.

And then there is, of course,
the issue of no little crossing-walk women,
say, in a skirt, with maybe the computer changing the
length of skirt to keep up with changes in fashion,
or, put her in pants,
with just a hint of boobs,
a few pixels on the computer,
may be all that is needed,
for a little crossing-walk woman.

And so who
made the little white crossing-walk man
white?

A racist sitting alone, gloating over his design,
or a committee, a conspiracy, working together to
favor their race in subtle yet powerful ways?

Or just some poor designer,
a victim of his culture,
who never saw the political
consequences of making the little white crossing-walk man
white.

Like a cabdriver with lots of
time on his hands
would have.

Or *her* hands I mean.
Of many colors.

Geese

Eduardo and I leaned against our cabs in holding, watching three planes coming in from the west just south of the volcanoes. A new guy was there with us, and he too leaned against his cab. Young, blond, short, and dumpy, he had already told us three times how tough he was, and twice how pretty his girlfriend was. Not that we cared.

"What do you think of that first plane?" I asked Eduardo.

He pushed away from his cab and walked a couple of paces to get a clear view.

"Hmmm . . ." he said, squinting and looking at the plane that was probably two miles away. "Delta. Riding a little low maybe. Say, three-quarters full."

"Businessmen, tourists, or homies?" I asked.

"Mostly businessmen, and a few tourists and homies. Most of the window shades are down. Businessmen don't care about scenery."

"And the second plane?"

Eduardo stared off at the next plane in line, probably four miles away. He pondered it for a moment.

"Well, that's a Southwest, wings not bowed at all, riding high, shades open, therefore mostly homies whose cars are in the parking garage. Probably nothing in there for us. Two, maybe three cabs go out. Not us. We're too far down the line."

"What do you think of that third plane?" Eduardo asked me. "Your eyes are better than mine." The third plane may have been eight miles out.

I walked over toward Eduardo, rubbing my chin. "Well, as I

see it, that is one big, fat goose stuffed full of money with our names on it." I pointed at the plane. "See there—look at that— that plane is riding so low, belly saggin,' wings bowed, with no lift and a lotta drag, that poor pilot is probably having trouble keeping it in the air. I see lots of tourists, maybe one-half to Old Town hotels putting twenty or more bucks in our pockets, three-quarters to downtown for fifteens, a couple runs to the pyramid for thirty or so, and the rest to points north, probably for Santa Fe or Taos. That how you read it Eduardo?"

"Exactly," he replied.

We both went back to leaning on our cabs, waiting for the radio to send us up.

"You guys are really good!" said the new guy.

"Just takes lots of practice," said Eduardo.

I nodded. ▨

Reverend Buckett

At the heart of a Sunday night I chose to abandon early
for want of work, or energy, I forget,
I idled for a moment or more in the shop before going home early,
casting my words like a broken chain of pennies,
or flat stones skipping on the water of a pond,
through the small half-circle of a hole in a smoky pane of glass
that separates the operators and dispatch from the riffraff of drivers
like me that pass.

And in the pause of the night, through that hole in
the smoky pane, I joked and flirted with the lovely Liz,
phone operator and high priestess,
in another lifetime or maybe this one I don't know,
and we spoke of her children and mine,
and my wife,
and Liz said I was lucky, even though she
had never met my wife, she could tell I was—

content.

and a lucky man,
and that she was pleased for me,
for finding strength with a woman,

because,

not all men find that strength, she said,

and without it the night will destroy a man if she wants to,
rip him from his life like a car wreck,
and cast the hearts of his loved ones on hot beach sands
to wither in the sun.

Liz spoke in her thick, wet, caramel voice,
her words like soft notes from a grieving cello,
played by Yo-Yo Ma at the bottom of a well.

With a passion only Western women have,
offering their young hearts and old souls and thoughts,
to those of us who will listen.

And these men they go down hard, she said,
like young John Buckett,
long, thin John Buckett,
Reverend John Buckett,
cabdriver John Buckett,
in his crisp, white shirt and tie,
only cabdriver I ever knew
wore a pressed shirt and tie,
hellfire and brimstone preacher on Sunday,
cabdriver on Saturday night,
children lined up like ducklings,
and a pretty wife in bright cotton,
dropping him off and picking him up
'cause they only had one car,
a shitty old Dodge.

And the night gobbled him up,
just like that.

His eyes grew dark in their sockets,
his veins grew thick,
he stumbled,
his shirt wrinkled and dirty,
eventually his heart too.
Cops caught him in an alley,
with some hooker's head in his lap,

and it made the papers,
photo of him in handcuffs and all,
'cause you know everyone loves a
preacher caught with his pants down,
and for him it was one foot in hell,
maybe more.

She sighed with sadness,
and shook her head,
like a sheepherder,
with a snake-bit lamb.

And we never saw him again,
after the story in the papers
but I hope he's on the up side,
or if not,
at least I hope his kids forgive him,
if not now

Someday.

Most men have tissue paper morals,
thin as the whiskey and beer they pour
down their gullets,
she said, raising her voice for all the
men in the shop, or maybe,
all the men in the world and beyond
to hear,
and wagging her finger at me,
if you have them at all.

and the night,
that goddam bitch,
she knows it.

Losing Traction

He didn't say that it was a drug run, but then they never do. It did, however, bear all of the characteristics of one. White guy, dressed nice, but not too nice. Thirtyish. Working class, not from here. East coast maybe. No gang marks or visible tracks. He had a nice little patter, a little chitchat, stroke the cabdriver a little, make him feel comfortable—I'd heard it all before. Of course, there is nothing like a fare getting into a cab and handing you a hundred-dollar bill to make you feel comfortable. But there were other signs that it was a drug run as well. Like the pick up at the 7-Eleven convenience store—but out of sight of all security cameras. Got in, handed me the bill, and gave me directions. No address. Drug dealers never give you an address. They just give you directions. And, when you are close to where they want you to go, they don't let you go to the actual house or apartment they are looking for. They get out, remind you that they will be right back and not to leave without them because they see a big tip in your future. They then walk down the street and around the corner to the crack house. And they take a bit of time, ten to twenty minutes or so. Then it is on to the next place. Same routine. Again and again, house to house, apartment to apartment. I'm not sure whether they are delivering, or just looking to buy and supply is low, and I never ask. And why are they in cabs, you might ask? Forfeiture laws. Get caught dealing or transporting in your own car, boat, or airplane, and you lose it. Get caught in a cab, no loss. Besides, you can toss the bag under the seat and insist you don't know anything about it if your cab is pulled over. Must have been some other passenger's stash.

This was our third stop. The hundred sat lightly in my pocket—dancing and grinning—at least it felt like it. Hundreds do that to me. Really. Franklin is like the Mona Lisa. Enigmatic grin. Lovely, inspiring, seductive.

The fare got out of my cab at Dakota north of Central, in the War Zone. Nasty mullet, I thought, as he started to walk away.

"Be right back," he said.

I nodded, put my parking lights on, electronically cranked all four windows near the top, locked the doors, turned down the radio, and put my foot down hard on the brake to remind myself I was still in drive. I never turn the engine off or put my cab in park in the War Zone. Park just doesn't feel comfortable here. I pulled my book off the dash. Billy Collins. The best. Look him up.

Lights hit my rearview, and I saw a police cruiser approach. They didn't even look at me as they drove by, pulling up to the stop sign half a block ahead of me. The car stopped, they looked around, and then pulled a few feet more into the intersection.

Two cops got out of the cruiser and went to its trunk. One black, one white. Big. Very Big. Both buff. Elite. Lifters *and* runners from the looks of it. Guys who took it seriously.

I sucked in my gut. For a moment, anyway. I flexed my pecs, or more correctly, what is left of them.

They opened the trunk, and the black guy pulled a sandbag out. The white guy opened it, and both men started spreading sand behind the car. Maybe a gallon of sand hit the street. After they kicked it around a bit, the cops climbed into the cruiser and pulled around the corner, rear wheels squealing slightly as they hit the sand and pulled away from the stop sign.

They parked where they could observe the stop sign, and sat and waited. I felt as much as saw lights in my rearview mirror. A car slid by me, driven by a young Latina with a couple of kids in car seats behind her. She pulled up to the stop sign, full stop, looked both ways, scolded the kids, then moved on. Her tires squealed as they hit the sand pulling away from the stop sign.

Lights went on the cruiser, and she pulled over, flashers popping on. The cops got out, took their time going through the car, then gave her a warning and let her go.

The cops returned to their position, and the next person to get pulled over after her tires squealed was an old lady. They searched her too, and wrote her a ticket for a broken taillight.

I watched for another twenty minutes or so, meter ticking, while three more cars were pulled over and searched. Finally, I saw my fare come around the corner, where he stood next to the curb and watched the police operation for two or three minutes. The cops waved him off, telling him this was none of his business. He walked over to my cab, shaking his head.

"Damn," he said, climbing into the cab. "That sucks."

"How can they pull them over?" I asked. "They were doing nothing wrong."

"Oh yeah they were," he said. "They were losing traction."

"Losing traction?"

"Yeah, losing traction. It's a traffic violation. Any time your tires squeal, you have lost traction, which means that in the eyes of the law you have lost control of your car, and it is a misdemeanor, and gives them an excuse to search your car."

"But the cops spread the sand out there by the stop sign," I said. "That's the only reason they are losing traction."

"Yeah, cops do it all the time. You know that. If they can't think of a reason to stop us, they make one up. Let's go. We have a couple more stops to make."

I pulled forward into the intersection slowly and stopped at the stop sign. Carefully. The cops looked at me. I looked back. I sat at the stop sign for a moment. I felt the sand beneath my tires.

"Don't even fuckin' think about it," said my fare.

I grinned and stepped on the gas. ▩

Vincent

Some cholo motherfucker
climbed into Vincent's backseat
and started beating him with
a half full or half empty (depending
upon your philosophy of life)
Jim Beam bottle that
had been hidden somewhere
in the great folds of a baggy
red and black
Chicago Bulls jacket.

Buckled in for safety (chained to a four
thousand pound yellow anchor),
the blows fell on Vincent's head,
shoulder, and raised right arm
'till just this side of forever
when a couple of crackwhores
working the Circle K at Central and
Pennsylvania heard the shouting
and ran the cholo off.

Twenty-seven stitches and a red
Lobos baseball cap to hide the scars later,
Vincent drives around with his left hand
on the grip of a palm-sized Kel-Tec P 32
semi-automatic, lock breached pistol
(no safety) with seven hollow point bullets
in the clip,

tucked neatly
under his right arm

pointed toward the cab's backseat

at you. ▨

Thankful

I coasted to a stop in front of Jesús's house. The night was over, and I was giving him a ride home, as I often do. Jesús had never owned a car in his life. "Too much money," he once told me. "And besides," he had added, "why does a cabdriver need a car when he is already leasing a cab for twelve hours a day?" He opened the door and started to pull his long, thin body out of my Crown Vic as dawn broke over the Sandias. I noticed that his long ponytail nearly reached the belt of his dirty Wranglers. Then he sat back down.

"*Gracias, amigo,*" he said, wiggling the door back and forth on its hinges. "Do I owe you anything, a few bucks, a little pot maybe?"

"*De nada,*" I replied, shaking my head and flicking my tired hand to indicate no thanks.

"Weird fuckin' night out there, no?" he said. "I mean, you see all those *loco* ambulances, lights flickering and all, and the cops, they're fuckin' everywhere, pulling everyone over man, and the *borrachos* weaving all over the place in their cars and runnin' into shit like the dumfucks they are, and that jumper there at the Big-I overpass, when the cops stopped everyone, and all those drunk college *pendejos* fighting downtown, and hey, did you see that girl lying in the middle of the street front of the Midnight Rodeo with all that blood around her head reflectin' in the moon and everythin'?"

"Full moon," I said. "It's always like this on the full moon."

He climbed out of the car and leaned on the sill of the open window. "You make any money, man?"

"A fistful."

"Me too," he said, pulling a wad of cash out of the pocket of his navy blue T-shirt. A toothy grin broke out on both sides of his long narrow nose. "I'm a rich man. A few good days here with this convention and I can buy lots of beer, maybe even good beer, pay my rent, take a real nice girl out to dinner if I want to. Not one of these young girls who know all about music I don't care about and just want to fuck and don't know my music from that MTV shit they all listen to, but a real woman, maybe a doctor or lawyer chick who knows who Charlie Parker was, maybe one who finds that they are all set in their jobs and careers and all that but just maybe they forgot to find a man along the way, or maybe found and lost one or two but no one pays them attention like they deserve and no one appreciates them, but here I am, man, interested in who they are and what they have to say even if I don't understand it all and they don't give a shit that I don't know what they're talkin' about 'cause I really care and don't have any trouble letting them know that even though the fact is that while they might think that cab driving really isn't a career it is sort of interesting anyway and maybe even romantic?"

"Good night," I said.

"*Buenas noches,*" he replied, but continued leaning against my car, still talking. "And I'm gonna go in my house and turn on TV and turn it to the news and I am going to sit there in my big fat chair, watch that hot blond newslady on Channel 7 and suck down a Pacifica or four or six and watch the news about all those poor fuckin' people out in the world who died last night in all those wars we don't belong in or on the street and shit and

I am going to thank our Lord that I am alive and thinkin' about the next girl about to be in my life I don't even know yet 'cause I am such a lucky man."

He took a breath. "And I'm gonna thank him too that you are alive and sit there all relaxed like and grin and just fuckin' be happy that we are alive after that piece a shit night we just drove through and more than that, I am going to say a prayer not only for you but for your *esposa* and your *niños* and for all those poor dead fuckers who didn't make it through the night, and then, and only then, after *muchas* Pacificas and prayers I will go to sleep and I will sleep so fuckin' well just like a teeny little baby because our Lord has showed that even if He wasn't there for everyone in the world last night you and I were near the top of His list 'cause He was there for us 'cause we aren't dead."

He shut the car door and waved, then pointed a finger at me.

"You gonna pray for me, *amigo?*"

"I don't pray," I said, pulling away and starting down the street toward home.

He smiled and waved and kicked at my car as I drove off, and I heard him yelling in the distance. "Well then, you poor ignorant *gringo* bastard, it's a goddam good thing you got someone like me saying his prayers for you!" ▤

Yankee

There's a time of the night,
when bar rush is over and the wake
of drunks calms,
a little,
and before the port runs begin,
when the hookers and dealers,

our non traditional capitalists of the night,
get restless, and take wing,
like moths on a hot summer's evening,
they batter themselves against the roving porchlight
that travels across the city, up and down
the arteries of Central, Route 66,
America's Highway,
purveyors of part of the pleasure that defines
the ability of many to get
their kicks,
on Route
66.

I help them chase the light I cannot always clearly see,
and don't necessarily want to follow,
but do,
because the money's good.

Our cabs are their conveyance,
though a lattice of wandering rubber-toothed cops,

as effective as Helen Keller with a badge,
well-intentioned or not,
but mostly not.

Whenever the entrepreneurs
of the night idle, and the world is dead empty,
gravity draws my India Indian
friend Saini and me together,
and we coast downhill to a vacant gravel and glass lot,
across from the Greyhound Bus Depot,

to talk.

Sometimes our conversations turn to
the ancient economy of the Harappan Civilization,
or the origins of Sanskrit,
or the versatility of the Urdu language
in matters of commerce.

And sometimes we just talk about women.

Tonight he asked me to explain
the cultural significance, to men my age,
of John Wayne.

My Indian friend, with his degree
in computer sciences,
who dreams of opening a restaurant,
or if he works hard enough—

and I can see him smiling now—
owning a gas station
in Moriarty on that ribbon of cash the unaware call I-40.

Mr. Saini, citizen who pondered the virtues of
all of the civilizations of the modern world and chose our country
above all others on the globe in which to live,
a choice of consequence, not luck, and arguably
more meaningful
than arriving as an accident of birth as most of us do.

My friend from India, with his dark skin and lovely accent,
who suffered repeatedly at the hands of our ignorant countrymen,
during the days following 9/11,

cleverly found safety
under the crisp, rounded brim of a brand new,
New York Yankees baseball cap
he bought at the mall. 🔲

Dreams

"Hey, leave her alone!" I yelled through my cab window at the collective scum bothering a girl standing near the curb at the bus station. The three guys dressed mostly in rags and dirt that were crowding the girl backed off as I left my cab swinging my big black mag light. When they scattered I grabbed her bag and threw it into the trunk as she climbed into the backseat and locked the door.

"Thanks," she said, when I climbed in and punched the meter. "For some reason those fellas thought I might wanna join 'em for the evening."

"Shitheads," I said. "Fucking bums."

"I think those guys might be what we're supposed to call *the* homeless," she said, laughing. "And they thought they had a real deal goin' for me—a warm spot to sleep betwixt 'em and a bottle to share."

"Optimists, and undeservedly so," I said, easing into traffic by the bus station. "Where do you want to go?"

"Well," she said, thinking about her options. "I suppose find me a hotel room for the night—but somewhere safe. I don't really need another offer from gentlemen like those fellas."

Shit, I thought. Another one of those crappy short runs from the bus to a cockroach-infested hotel on Central near downtown. Tourists loved the neon-lit hotels on old historic Route 66, but not enough to stay there. They thought them "quaint" and historical. They didn't know that most of them would have been condemned a century ago in Calcutta. "How much you want to spend?" I asked.

"Hmmmm. . . . Can I get a decent place for, say, fifty bucks?" I felt my hopes rising. This girl had money and didn't want to sleep in a dump tonight. A fifty-dollar hotel was at least a twelve-buck fare away. I could live with that.

I pulled to a stop at the red light at Second and Gold. "Sure," I said. I turned and looked at her to make sure she wasn't a crazy. I had, after all, only seen a glimpse of her at the bus station. She saw me glance at her and smiled back at me. My heart warmed. She was safe. No druggie or nutcase. She reminded me of Winona Ryder before she was a thief. Her accent told me west Texas. "There are a couple of hotels near the airport that will cost that," I said. "You want me to run you out there?"

"Well that sounds real nice and all, but that's a bit away from where I need to be. Could you get me over to the east part of the city—I have friends who I can call to pick me up to go home to Moriarty tomorrow. I just don't want to bother them at three in the morning." My mind pictured the long run to Moriarty, a small town just off the Interstate about forty miles east of town, and inspiration hit.

"You know, I can get you to Moriarty for fifty bucks. The meter will say seventy-five or eighty, but you give me fifty now we'll be there before you could punch the hotel remote enough times to find HBO." She didn't say anything, but I knew what was on her mind—is this guy safe? Can I trust him to drive me through the stinking desert in the middle of the night? Is he a crazy? Is he going to leave me for dead lying in the middle of a bunch of jackrabbits and snakeweed?

I waited for the conversation to pause on my radio then keyed it. "Two forty-six."

"Two forty-six?" replied Jerry the dispatcher, giving me the cue that communication was open.

"A pretty young lady in the backseat is thinking about riding to Moriarty with me. She's about half my age and half my size. Do you believe that she has anything to worry about?"

The radio sat silent for a moment. "He's the closest thing we've got to a gentleman driving tonight, ma'am," said Jerry.

Laughter erupted in the backseat as I turned right at the Sunshine Theater. About the time I passed under the railroad tracks crossing over Central, I heard the crisp sound of cash being counted in the backseat. When I heard a pause in the counting, I put my hand back over my shoulder and two twenties and a ten filled it. I pulled out my money clip—actually a paper binder clip, counted the money again, folded the bills into the rest of my money, and slipped it into my shirt pocket neatly behind my cell phone. I tapped it to make sure it was still there. I tapped it again just in case as I ripped past the cheap motels on Central, popped out under the freeway, and without hitting a light I turned left hitting the ramp and merged onto a middle-of-the-night freeway where she and I were alone in the world for the next forty minutes or so.

My engine roared as I pushed the gas pedal nearer the floorboard as we climbed the mountain at the edge of town. I thumbed my radar detector volume to high and turned the radio down and settled in for conversation, if she would have any.

"You from Moriarty?" I asked.

"No, just live there. Got me a real nice doublewide on half a section just south of town." I could hear pride in her voice.

"Not many jobs in Moriarty, are there?"

"Few to none."

"So, if there are no jobs, what do you do there?"

"Well, to be honest, I'm seldom there, but when I am there's not much to do but get drunk or high and watch the boys fight if there's nothin' good on the satellite. Those boys there sure like to fight, and a young girl like me draws attention even if she don't want it, and well, to tell ya the truth, sometimes the guys seem more interested in fightin' than lovin'. But anyway, I keep tellin' 'em I got a boyfriend that drives a tank for the Bushies in Iraq, but that doesn't stop 'em from snortin' and spittin' and fightin' and showin' off hopin' to get a bit of my affection."

"So, if you're not from there, and don't work there, how did you wind up in Moriarty?"

"Believe it or not, saw it from the side of the road driving through and knew I had to have a place there. I was born in San Diego, my dad in the military. Moved around a lot when I was a kid, but when Mom died when I was nine we moved to Lubbock so my gramma could help raise me." She drew a breath and slowly exhaled. "God, I'd love to see my dad again."

"Well then get on the bus for Lubbock. What is it, a six-hour ride? That's not far." We crested the peak of the Sandias before she spoke.

"Not far for you. It's far for me because I've been disowned. My gramma got pissed when I graduated from high school and went and joined a carnival. Daddy lissens to his mama just like he is a scared little boy and there I am disowned sure as ya know it. Gramma said, 'Honey,' waggin' her finger at me, 'don't you dare come back here ever again as long as you hang with those lowlife carnival folk.' And she don't know nothin' about the carnival. I don't even think she's ever been."

I knew at least part of the answer to this question before I
asked it. That didn't stop me from asking it anyway. "So why
don't you quit the carnival and go home?"

The moon passed out from behind one cloud and into
another before she spoke.

"A girl can't listen to her gramma forever—besides, carnival
is big business now, not a bunch of lowlifes like they might have
been in the fifties when Gramma was growin' up. They are nice
people, and carnival is legit now—as legit as Haliburton anyway.
That carnival bought me my doublewide and the land it sets on
and I got forty-seven thousand dollars in the bank I been savin'
since high school. I run something called the Big Drop. Drops
people from seventy-five feet high at fifty-five miles per hour.
Ticket costs twenty-five bucks. Tosses eight people at a time. Two
hundred fifty people an hour when it's busy, twenty-five or so
when it's not. You do the math. Not much that is legal pays a girl
with a high school education that much when you consider fifty
percent goes to the owner for profit and setup and two other guys
and I pocket the rest after expenses."

"That is a lot of money," I said. She ignored me.

"Besides," she said, "this here carnival is my inspiration—the
travel, the people, the stimulation of bein' on the move, meetin'
new people, seein' new things—I have to have it—it's like a drug.
Don't know what I'd do without my inspiration. Wither and die,
I expect."

"Inspiration for what?"

"I write songs."

"They any good?"

"Well, maybe a hundred of 'em are good. Maybe a few more . . ." I heard her shift in her seat, and her tone changed, growing excited. "You like country western music?"

Not wanting to tell the truth, I responded, "Well, I grew up listening to Hank Williams and Patsy Cline . . ."

She sounded disappointed. "I expect then you don't know this group—let's just say they are pretty famous, have a record in the top ten on the country list every six or eight months or so, and have for ten years maybe. They were one of the headline acts playin' the Minneapolis State Fair last year, and I really like them, and so when I saw a few of the guys from the band wanderin' the midway there I said, 'Hey boys, take yourselves a free ride here on the Big Drop, and mention it durin' the concert tonight would ya to drum up us some more business?'

"And so a few of them took the drop, had fun, and afterwards we were jokin' around, and the girl bass player in the band said, 'Hey, if you want to stop by the bus and see us later, come on by,' and so I did. It was about two in the mornin' when their concert was over and the midway was closed and so I wandered over to their bus and knocked on the door and some guy I hadn't seen before said, 'Come on in girl, heard you might be stoppin' by,' and then it came to me he was the lead singer, and that he just seemed a bit more handsome on CMT—that's Country Music Television—than in real life right there before me leanin' outta the bus and all, and so I went in and sat down and someone handed me a Coors and before you knew it the guy passin' out beers asked me if I played, and I said, a little, yeah. Buster the steel guitar player said, 'What do you play?' And I said just about anythin' 'cause it don't take me long to figure my way around an instrument 'cause my daddy was in a band and he taught me some.' I let 'em know that only once had I ever been bothered a bit about an instrument and that was the harmonica, but after a couple weeks practice when I was twelve I don't sound bad, but that I prefer the guitar if given a choice. And then the big star of the group came over and gave me his own guitar—can ya believe it—his *own* guitar—and said, 'Hey honey, play us a little somethin' then.' And I was real nervous, and wondered about what to play for a second or two, but then I figured that I had better play somethin' I know real well, so I picked one of my songs, and by the end of it the rest of the band had joined in and we were all playin' and somehow it just sounded real good—to me anyhow. Well, I guess it worked for them too because at the end of the song we all whooped an' hollered a bit and cleared our throats with another Coors and then the boss said, 'Hey girl, you're a real fine picker and singer but what I really want to know is where you heard that song.' And then I said I wrote it and he said, 'You got any more songs as good as that?' and so I played a few more of my favorite songs I wrote with the band, and when that was over, they were all grinnin' and laughin' and pattin' me on the back and the boss man said something like, 'Hey girl you are really good.' And then he went to a corner and talked with this old man that wasn't really dressed country but had a nice smile, and after a few minutes the old man and the boss came over and they offered me a job with the band—and I'm for sure not shittin' you—and when they heard that the rest of the band hooted and hollered again and when that stopped the old man told me that if I might be interested they just might want to record some of my songs if I had others as good as the three or four we did.

"And I was really thrilled—as you might imagine—but told them that I had a commitment to the carnival for the next eight months—that I had made a promise to the boss who had treated me well, and that I was sorry, but I was goin' to honor that because my word is my bond. Well, the band respected that they did, and the old man said, 'When that eight months is over, you join us girl.' And I said I would. And the next mornin' I told my boss at the carnival what had happened, and he said, 'You be crazy girl—you don't owe me nothin'. You go with that band and you make us all proud.' But I told him my word is my bond, and that I will keep it just like my daddy and Gramma taught me. And so to make a long story short, in three months from now, the band and I are meetin' up in Nashville after the Tennessee State Fair to play for awhile, and if we come up with somethin' good, we're gonna record it. And then even if it works out and I want to stay with them and they want me aroun' for a while they got no problem with me doin' carnival now and again 'cause they know and appreciate the fact that I need inspiration. But, this time next year, I'll be in a country western band, and if my songs are any good, we'll be recordin' them, and I want you to turn on a country station now and again and listen for me on the radio, driver."

She tapped me on the shoulder and pointed at an exit sign. Moriarty. I swerved toward it. I had almost missed the turnoff, but thanks to her warning had caught it. I acted like I had consciously chosen to hit the exit at eighty-five miles an hour and that she hadn't needed to remind me.

"How old are you?" I asked, pumping the brakes gently.

"Just turned twenty-one."

My speed corrected, I pulled into Moriarty, obeying the

small-town speed limit. She pointed at the Chevron gas station on the west edge of town with its all-night restaurant and truck stop.

"I can walk from there. I need to stretch my legs after the trip, and I think I'll grab a bite first."

I pulled to a stop just short of the gas pumps and out of the way of the big rigs, close to the restaurant.

I climbed out of the cab, popped the trunk, and pulled her bag out. She joined me behind the car and took it. I slammed the trunk shut, and then looked her full in the face for the first time. "Think your dad and Gramma will forgive you for having joined the carnival once you are a famous country western singer and songwriter?"

She smiled. "I plan to be home for Christmas next year," she said. "Already bought the ticket."

She reached into her pocket and handed me another twenty. It was a crisp, brand-new one. "That there's your tip, driver."

"Thanks, Miss."

She started walking away then turned. "You be sure to follow your dreams too, ya hear?"

I nodded and climbed back into my cab. I watched her walk safely into the restaurant before I pulled away, pointing west toward the city, and my dreams. ▨

Lucifer

Miniature whirlwinds of steam swirled out of the square hole in the lid of my styrofoam Circle K coffee cup. I took a sip. The heat bit my upper lip as the hot coffee splashed onto my tongue, stalled momentarily, cooled infinitesimally, and finally rushed down my throat. I felt the now-warm coffee gravitate downward to contact my stomach lining, and consciously studied the feeling as the temperature of the coffee reached the temperature of the remainder of the contents of my stomach.

I slumped in my seat, parked at the Circle K at Candelaria and Tramway, staring west at the moonlit city below me. My engine popped and creaked as it cooled on a mild summer night, and I watched red and white cop lights flash at a dozen or more locations over the vast expanse of Albuquerque below me. I was reading the fine print on the coffee cup when the sound of the radio broke the silence.

"Two forty-six," said Jerry the dispatcher.

I grabbed my mike, startled, nearly spilling my coffee. It had been over an hour since my last call, and the radio had been silent for at least twenty minutes. I looked at the time. 3:15 a.m.

"Two forty-six," I replied, hurriedly putting my coffee cup between my legs. I grabbed my notepad and fumbled with my pen, getting ready to write down an address if I needed to.

"I have a personal for you. You and only you."

Good deal, I thought. Personals were normally calls from regulars who liked riding with you, and were often good money. That or they could be family or friends. I hoped it was the former as family and friends often don't want to pay or don't have the money. Plus it feels weird asking them for it.

"It's a corner call."

I put my pen down. Corner calls were the most dangerous calls there were. No address to trace, no security cameras. Just someone standing alone in the dark, maybe with a stolen cell phone in their hand and their mind on a cabdriver's take for the night.

"Where?" I asked.

"Corner of Bell and Indiana."

Damn. The part of town even the mayor calls the War Zone. A river of drugs flows into a river of blood in the War Zone, and my thoughts turned to the bodies I had seen lying in the streets over the years. But it's work, I thought, and there are regular people in the Zone who just might need a ride.

I started the cab and put it in gear. I spoke into the mike as I lifted my foot off the brake.

"Who is it for?" I asked, going over possible routes in my mind. Let's see, scoot down Tramway to Central, down to San Pedro . . .

"Man says his name is Lucifer."

I put my foot back on the brake and keyed the mike.

"Let me get this straight. I have a personal—a corner call—in the War Zone, for Lucifer?"

The radio was silent for a moment.

"That's right."

I put the car back into park.

"I think I'll pass."

"Thought you would." 🔲

The White Man

I walked down the dirty, brown hallway between the garage and the dispatch office to the cashier's cage. It was time for the six o'clock night drivers to come on and for the day drivers to come off shift. I was a little early. I rounded the corner to the cage and saw the broad back of someone ahead of me in line. Blue jeans, black T-shirt, black engineer boots, and the sagging shoulders of a man who had been worked hard. His shaved, pink head glistened under the flourescent lights of the shop.

"How are you, Troy?" I asked as he finished counting out his lease money to pay Bill the cashier. "Ninety-two, ninety-three, ninety-four . . ." He reached into his pocket and slapped a handful of change on the counter. I heard coins sliding on Formica. "Ninety-four seventy-six. That should do it."

He turned and looked at me and nodded. "Doin' OK I guess, for a white man in a brown man's world."

I leaned against the counter. "What does that mean?"

"First, it means I'm sick. I've spent every day I'm not working for the past coupl'a days sitting in the waiting room at the University Hospital. I walk in and stand in line for an hour. When I get to the receptionist she asks me what's wrong. I say I don't know. I'm sick. Inside. I need to see a doctor. She asks me if I have insurance. I say no. She asks me how I expect to pay for it. I say I don't know—depends on how much it costs. She hands me some paperwork. I fill it out and hand it to her. She looks all bored—filing her nails and shit—and says for me to wait. I wait for six hours. All the white people wait. Everyone that's brown, they walk in, stand in line, and in a little bit some doctor sees them. If they speak Spanish and don't understand English, someone helps them with their paperwork and then a doctor sees them."

Bill staples Troy's gas ticket and lease receipt together and passes the paperwork through the half-circle cut in the safety glass window that separates drivers from the cashier.

"Thank you, sir," says Troy, folding the papers over once and then slipping them into his back pocket. He slips a dollar tip to Bill. Bill is listening now.

"After six hours I ask if I am going to get to see a doctor. A different receptionist says they need to see my bank statement. Give them evidence of bank activity for the past two months, she says. I say the bank is closed. She says come back tomorrow then. The next morning I feel like shit. I wait till the bank opens. Get my bank statement with evidence of two months of activity. Go to the hospital again. Wait in line. I give them my bank statement. They make me wait again. More brown people get to see a doctor. I speak some Spanish, ya know. So I ask a few people in Spanish if they are from the U.S. or Mexico. Some are from Mexico. I ask if they have insurance. They laugh. I ask if they are paying for this. They say no—they don't have any more money than I do. They ask me if I have to pay for it, and I say I guess so. They're not real happy about that either, but they get to see the doctor. All the white people but one pregnant girl that someone had beat the shit out of wait. She gets to see a doctor. About noon I ask the receptionist if I get to see a doctor. What do you think happens?"

I shuffle my feet a bit, then shift my weight and lean on the other elbow. I am embarrassed for reasons I don't understand. "You wait some more?" I ask.

"Well, yeah, that too. But first she says that my bank statement says I don't have very much money. I say I know that. She says sometimes you have money, sometimes you don't, and you don't have any now. I say I know that. More brown people get to see the doctor. One old white guy gets to see the doctor. And guess what happens now?"

His gaze is discomforting. I wonder if I am turning pink. I look at the clock in the cashier's cage, then at Bill. He shrugs his shoulders from behind the glass. "You wait some more?"

"Well, yeah, that too. But first the receptionist says somebody upstairs needs to see your tax return. I say I don't carry around copies of my tax return. She says go get it. So I go home. Get my tax return. Go to Kinko's and make a copy. I go back to the hospital, and wait in line. More brown people get to see a doctor. All the same white people are still waiting. About eight at night I ask if I get to see a doctor. The receptionist says no, not today. Come back tomorrow. That is today. Tomorrow is today I mean. But I need to work. You need to work?" He waits for me to answer.

"I need to work. Sure I need to work. We all need to work," I said. "You need to work, Bill?" I asked. Bill nods.

"Sure, everyone needs to work," said Troy. "So I come in this morning and get my cab. I drive it to the hospital. Park it. Then I stand in line. When I get to the window the receptionist—same one—she says wait. Lots of brown people get to see the doctor. A couple of white people leave without seeing a doctor. About noon I ask if I get to see a doctor. The receptionist says she doesn't know, but will check. In a few minutes some lady that isn't a receptionist comes out and tells me that my bank activity for the past two months doesn't 'fit well' with my tax return. I say of course not. I am a cabdriver. Nothing matches anything. I cheat on my taxes. So what if my taxes say I have even less than the no money that I have in the bank? I ask am I going to get to see the doctor or not? She says she doesn't know. She tells me to wait awhile. Pissed, I walk out. Climb in my cab. Pay eight dollars for parking. I take a call. I keep taking calls. I needed to work to make my lease. I worked till a few minutes ago. I made my gas, my lease, and I have about twelve dollars to take home. And here I am, talking to you, and I still haven't seen a doctor but maybe half the population of Mexico has and all the rest of the brown people in town."

He stops talking.

"I'm sorry," I said.

"Me too. I think I'm dying, man." 🔳

The Tattoo Dance

At OPM
Mahogany barroom double doors
faced with bright chrome knobs
and hinges,
spring open at closing time
like gates at the dog track
and the instant they part,
the sleek greyhounds explode
to chase the mechanical rabbit,
really nothing more
than a fur-covered lie moving
just a touch faster than the dog,
and the first wave of the crowd
is gone, into the night.
Dog lungs bursting in
pursuit of the rabbit that will
catch them.

Eventually.
Then a pause,
and the second wave slips
through, onto the slick asphalt
sidewalk, rising above it at first,
then fanning out, only to settle,
like ducks alighting
on a glassy pond,
languidly, ready to
engage, in ancient rituals
of courtship,

mitigated, and facilitated
by ink.

One couple converses, then
his eyes alight, on a small Chinese
dragon,
perched, where the curve of her neck
fades into breast.
Her eyes give permission, then a finger
touches, ever so lightly, in appreciation
and in wonder, as if contemplating a miniature
Matisse, then he retreats, respectfully, demurely,
awaiting her next invitation.

Another young man holds a slender brown wrist,
and inspecting an illustrated rose, he bends to taste its aroma,
and she smiles, then turns and offers a shoulder
adorned by the Virgin, a cloaked Madonna, eyes
focused downward, and when he sighs at her beauty—
their beauty—she smiles, her eyes close, and she arches her spine,
placing her slender hands on her thighs, thumbs inward,
offering the small of her back for his inspection, her Levi's tightening
below a tribal glyph, she trustingly presents her rump.

As do her sisters of savannah,
and jungle. ▦

Confined

"Drivers, let me talk to two twenty-five and *only* two twenty-five," said Butch the dispatcher.

Since we could only hear the dispatcher's side of the conversation, more than one driver might key his mike to speak only to "walk on" another driver. Someone was "walking on" two twenty-five.

Butch paused to listen, and the radio cleared for two twenty-five.

A moment passed.

"No, you are correct," said Butch, "I didn't mention that the fare would be *confined to a wheelchair.*"

He paused again before speaking, this time with irritation in his voice.

"Well, *you* may consider him 'confined to a wheelchair' if you want to. I prefer to think of it as the wheelchair providing the man a means of escaping the confinement of his house, a magnificent vehicle through which he manages to obtain freedom."

A pause.

"Now, two twenty-five, are you going to pick him up, or stand in the man's way? . . .

"I thought so." 🔳

New Guy

I choked the mike like I was strangling a goose, screaming into it, only to be ignored by Jerry the dispatcher. I imagined him sitting behind the big board fiddling with our pegs, and laughing. I might have well been broadcasting from the moon into a teacup. No way was he going to hear me or anyone else except when the spirit moved him. It seemed as if a thousand calls were available, and I couldn't catch one. The problem was some shithead new guy was clogging the radio. Since it was a training night for him, Jerry was being patient, and didn't say anything about his long-winded responses to a simple call. I could tell from the radio that other drivers were beginning to get pissed, as one driver taking up too much radio time on a busy night also took money from our pockets—we couldn't take calls when we wanted, it would take longer to service calls, and frustrated fares would turn into no-shows and cancellations. It's not hard to answer a dispatcher's call, repeat an address, and log into a zone. It can be crisply accomplished in a few seconds and this guy was taking a lot longer than that. Even worse, he didn't know the city, and didn't have a map, saying he couldn't afford one. As a result, Jerry had to hold the guy's hand through every call from dispatch to doorbell. Surprisingly, Jerry kept his patience this night, and might for a few more. After one long set of directions from Jerry, and an extended discussion to get to an address everyone else knew, the new guy finally made it to the right address.

"Stick with me kid," said Jerry, "and I'll make a rocket surgeon out of you yet." 🔳

Inspiration

Being a night driver
is a good job for a poet.
Twelve hours spent pressed
into the blue seat of a Yellow Cab,
mostly Naugahyde, rubber, and steel,
pierced by synthetic veins carrying
torrents of hydraulic fluids, coolants,
gasses, and greasy oils
that pulse and cook,
held together by the hopes of
a seven-dollar-an-hour mechanic
(yes, they do exist),
and powered by the detonations
of billions of diminutive suns,
just a little to the right of the
gas pedal and beyond.

While through the backseat,
nestled intimately behind
one's right shoulder, ready
to whisper or bellow into one's ear
passes all of humanity,
its dregs and delights,
rich man poor man,
young woman old woman,
and some genders beyond,
maybe from a galaxy far, far away,
they pass in staccato chorus line,
through a shared bench backseat,

a circus parade of imagination,
a fleshy river of inspiration
and experience revealed
in pure, sweet anonymity
in the grip of the night,
as the city roars,

then purrs,
languidly settling
its big body,
curling in on itself
pausing only to offer
vast, oozing spans of time,
great gobs of buttery time,
for the poet to guzzle
trapped in the belly
of the yellow beast.
and in that void,
and without warning,
thoughts erupt
like grapeshot from a cannon,
and if we're lucky,
before those unfettered thoughts
slip away,
to that magical place where
all lost thoughts go,
sometimes we write them down.

like now.

Just Leave

Hey all you rude, smartass, dirt-talkin', "tough" guys from New York City who hate the desert, complain about our restaurants, the quality of the club scene, the wages, the price of cabs, callin' our women dogs, and wouldn't know a green chile if I slapped you on the top of your chunky head with one. Don't let the door of my Yellow Cab hit you on the ass when I drop you off at the airport on your way outta here, and just remember as you head out that if you can't make it here you can't make it anywhere. ▣

Bootstraps

The other night,
as the wind howled
and rocked my parked cab,
and the streetlamp
lit the snowflakes
as they skittered
across my windshield
like a million dancing
miniature bonfires,
I cranked up the heater,
took a sip of fresh, hot
7-Eleven coffee,
and felt the thick wad of cash
from a busy night
and what seemed like
a thousand fares in my
shirt pocket,
I knew all was right
with the world.

Until I noticed a homeless man
wrapped in cardboard and hope,
huddled out of the wind
with his arms around
and cheek to cheek
with his German shepherd,
in a storefront at about
Fifth and Central.

Uncomfortable with all
the inequity in the world,
like the good liberal I am,
I sat up in my seat,
put my coffee in its holder,
and the PRNDL3L2 in D,
and drove around the
block to find a more
comfortable place
to park,
near the Hyatt.

Had I been a conservative,
I suspect that I would have
at least contemplated giving the man
a lecture on initiative,
the importance of hard work,
and of pulling himself up
by his own bootstraps

before I drove away,
snow crunching beneath
my tires. ▦

Volunteers

Bar rush was nearly over, and only a few drunken stragglers wandered the streets. I sat parked at Fourth and Central hoping to catch a last stray with cash. I could use a long run to the double R, but would take anything. A few calls were going out in other parts of town, but nothing for me. I sat and waited with the patience only cabdrivers and lifers-in-prison have. I was watching a few leaves rocking in the gutter, nudged by a gentle summer breeze, when I saw cab 222 approaching. It pulled up beside me, and the driver rolled down the window.

"How's it going?" the driver asked, pulling to a stop. He was a new guy I had seen a couple of times, but had never spoken with. Slender, middle-aged, in plaid, with a mullet.

"Not bad," I replied, not conveying any real information. If I told him the truth, that I was doing great, he would think that I was bullshitting him. Or worse, as a new guy he would listen to the radio and try to figure out what I was doing and copy my strategy and cut into my business. On the other hand, if I told him that I wasn't doing well, he would think that he was a better driver, and therefore man, than me, and I couldn't have that. Not with a new guy anyway. We only told our good buddies the truth, and that only some of the time.

He climbed out of his cab, leaned against it, lit a cigarette, and offered me one. I declined it with a flick of my wrist. A couple of low riders and an old green Chevy pickup passed by us. That was the second, no, the third time for the pickup. I tried to look inside, but tinted windows didn't give me the opportunity.

A pretty girl in her mid-twenties stumbled out from the plaza between Raw and Maloney's. She wobbled in her heels, and the weight of her pocketbook seemed to make her list to one side. Coming off the curb toward us, she stumbled out of her heels, cursed, then picked them up and tucked them under her arm next to her bag. She continued, walking barefoot in our direction in a short black skirt and tube top.

"Nice legs," said the other driver.

I nodded.

She touched her hair, and with more effort than she cared to exert pulled up a smile from somewhere deep down inside her, and directed it at me from about thirty feet away. Momentarily it fell away as if she had forgotten that she might need it.

"Looks like you got one," he said.

"If I do, I don't think I want it," I replied.

She came up between our cabs, ignored him, and leaned on mine. She was probably very attractive in real life, but her eyes were dull and cheeks flaccid in this world. She mumbled something that was unintelligible, and half a nipple peaked out at me from the edge of her tube top.

She may have said something about a ride.

"Nothing personal," I said, "but I need to see some money."

She stared at me without recognition of what I had said, then stared at her purse, then back at me. A synapse fired.

"Fuck you," she said, fairly intelligibly, hitting my cab with a shoe and a throaty grunt. She staggered west.

"Keep walking," I said loudly out of my window. "Five blocks, if you can count that high. Hotel Blue. It's safe and they'll let you use the phone if you don't vomit on the desk clerk."

In my rearview mirror I watched her stumble toward the Blue, and when she was two blocks away, a black and white unit pulled up and the policeman inside started talking with her.

"You called that one right," said the mullet.

"Happens all the time. You'll get used to it."

The Chevy pickup passed again.

"What are these guys doing circling around?" the new guy asked.

"They're vultures," I replied, pulling out my thermos to pour some coffee.

He raised an eyebrow.

"These guys and others like them show up about fifteen minutes before closing time, look for drunk girls wandering the streets, sloppy drunk girls whose dates or girlfriends left them behind, girls who don't have enough money for cab fare, act like they had talked to them in the bars, and then try to get them to climb in."

A sad look that was almost a shudder passed through the new guy. We sat for a few moments, watching two more drunk girls wander around, then bump into each other and ricochet different directions.

The silence was broken by the radio.

"Two twenty-two." It was Butch calling the mullet.

"Two twenty-two." he replied, letting Butch know he was listening.

"Just checkin' your vitals," said Butch. "Hadn't heard from you in a while."

"I'm fine, I guess. Just sitting here at Fourth and Central with two forty-six watching broke, drunk, half-naked girls wandering around about to get into some real trouble."

"Yeah, too bad," said Butch. "They're out there nearly every night. Sad thing is those poor girls aren't victims—they're volunteers."

We sat there for a few moments, and in my rearview mirror I saw that the cop had let the girl who had talked to me continue up the street.

"Well, I'm gonna save one of them," said the new guy, climbing into his cab and putting it into gear. ▣

The American Dream

Bill,
the weekend night dispatcher,
huddles over the big board
in his white T-shirt and Wranglers,
moving our numbered yellow pegs
and the mike foot pedal,
as he puts out calls between
puffs on his Pall Malls.

He pulls calls from
the chute that come
written on little paper sleds,
for twelve hours
straight
each Friday
and Saturday night
from 7 to 7.

During the week,
he's a day driver,
fighting syrupy traffic,
a mischievous sun,
and weary cops
who won't cut a
working man a break.

Before Bill gets into his cab

for his twelve-hour shift
as a day driver, he throws newspapers,
The Albuquerque Journal,
five mornings a week from 3 to 5 a.m.
During the hollow of the night,
when its belly is empty,
we learn a lot over the radio from Bill
like if the forecast is for clear weather,
he wraps each paper in a rubber band,
twisted twice, before the toss.

And if it has rained, or if rain is predicted
(or if he just feels it in his bones,
or smells it)
he inserts the paper in a plastic
bag before each toss,
which is actually much more efficient,
ergonomically,
than twisting rubber
bands.

Bill's wife throws the newspapers
the other two nights of the week,
while he's behind the big board,
to pick up the slack. He feels
bad that it is his wife,
rather than him,
that has to toss the
fat Sunday.

In his spare time,
he loves to drink beer,
and use his new
smoker to smoke meat
for his family and friends
(anything dead can be smoked,
according to Bill),

and to study Bollinger bands,
to help him make his
investment decisions
as he juggles money
on Scott e-trade on the
Internet,
the poor man's portal
to the stockmarket
and the

American Dream.

765 La Vega on a Saturday Night

Bill the dispatcher
says,

765 La Vega . . .
765 La Vega . . .
765 La Vega . . .

every two or three
minutes,
for an hour or so.

765 La Vega . . .
765 La Vega . . .
765 La Vega . . .

April has such a
soft,
pretty,
voice.

She wants to go
downtown, to
Second and Gold
to party a bit.

765 La Vega . . .
765 La Vega . . .
765 La Vega . . .

I'm sure she looks lovely
sitting on her front porch
waiting for someone
to pick her up.

765 La Vega . . .
765 La Vega . . .
765 La Vega . . .

Won't someone please
go pick up
April?

765 La Vega . . .
765 La Vega . . .
765 La Vega . . . ▨

Listen Up

"All right, drivers, listen up," said Butch the dispatcher to twenty-five drivers wandering the world on a rainy Friday night. Through my sweeping wiper blades I saw that sleet was beginning to mix with the rain. Another degree-or-two drop in the temperature would turn the wet streets into a giant ice skating rink. If the temperature dropped quickly, within the next half hour or so, it would be just in time for the drunks to erupt from the bars and rocket around in their cars in a terrible, bloody Ice Capade.

The radio was quiet momentarily as Butch waited for us to focus. Perhaps ten seconds passed, but it seemed longer. He really wanted us to listen. Finally he spoke.

"Here is the deal. The phone operator got a phone call she didn't know what to do with and passed it to me. Some guy wanted to know if our drivers were armed, and if cabdrivers made very much money."

He paused again.

"So watch your backs tonight, drivers."

The radio remained silent. Someone must have asked the question we all wanted to ask because he spoke again after a moment passed.

"I told him drivers don't make much money, and the little we do make we drop off regularly at the shop or at an ATM that takes deposits."

Another pause.

"And that all of you are packin' . . . sidearms . . . knives . . . and bad attitudes."

Another lengthy pause.

"And that all the cabs have big enough trunks to hold several fellas if they need to—and that we have shovels here at the shop." ▩

Disney World

Lovely little Maria,
in her daring red beret,
white cotton blouse,
short denim skirt,
and red vinyl heels,

uses her brown eyes,
bright smile,
long legs,
and TV sitcom
good looks and personality,

to help raise money
for her nephew Fernando's
school trip to Disney World,

by lifting her skirt
at Third and Central,

for two bucks
a peek. 🔳

Long Walk

Rounding the corner of Louisiana and Central, I was about ten miles above the speed limit when I punched in the phone number Butch had given me over the radio. Hard. Three no-shows in a row, and two nasty drunks I had to pull out of the backseat to the curb, had me in an intolerant mood.

"Hello?" said a deep voice at the other end. A little tipsy, but not too bad, I thought.

"You call a cab?" I asked.

"You're late."

The call had come out two minutes ago, and I was four, maybe five minutes away from the address.

"I'm not late. I don't take a call if I'm going to be late."

"Bullshit. Get your ass over here right now or I'll have your job."

I smiled and changed lanes, ready to head back to the airport.

"You heading somewhere important tonight?"

"Yeah, why?"

"Let me guess, is it downtown?"

"Cut the bullshit. You better be close."

"It's a simple question. Is it downtown?"

"Yes, dammit . . ."

"Well, you are going to be late. It's a long walk from your house to downtown." I started to hang up, but heard his voice before I could find the "end" button.

"What, you aren't coming?" I heard incredulity in his voice.

"Fuck no. The world is full of assholes. You did me a favor letting me know you're an asshole before you even got into the cab. Not only am I not coming, but I'm going to make sure that no one comes for you tonight, and if I feel ornery when I call it in, your address will be put on the no-cab list and you'll never get a cab again."

"That's not right . . ."

"No. It's called karma. It's as right as right gets. What's not right is you being rude. I don't like rude people, and I wouldn't subject another driver to your rude ass. Good bye." I started to hang up again.

"Wait!"

"What?"

"I really need a ride!"

"What makes you think I give a shit? You gotta learn to be polite."

"Really! I didn't mean anything!"

I heard a voice in the background. A feminine one.

"Ah . . . I get it. There's a girl there—a woman, your wife, no . . . probably your girlfriend . . . no, it's a date, right?"

"Yeah . . ."

"And you were showing off, being Mr. Tough Guy, trying to impress the girl, right?"

"I guess so . . . maybe . . ."

"She a new girl, or a girl you have known for awhile?"

"New."

"OK, then here is what you say if you want a ride. Ready to listen?"

"Yes."

"I want you to say, 'Sorry sir, I didn't mean to be rude. It is out of character for me and I apologize.' Now say it."

He hesitated.

"Say it."

"I'm sorry sir, I didn't mean to be rude. It is out of character for me and I apologize. Really."

"Now say to the girl, 'Sorry, (whatever her name is), I can't believe I did that. It was disrespectful to the driver, and to you.' Say it so I can hear it."

Nothing.

"Say it."

"Sorry, Ruth, I can't believe I did that. It was disrespectful to the driver, and to you."

Her voice lifted. I heard her say, "Thank you—it's OK."

I interrupted.

"Now you know that it doesn't pay to be rude to your cabdriver?"

"Yes, sir, that is correct."

"Say it won't happen again."

"It won't happen again."

"So, from now on, you won't be rude to mothers, grandmothers, or cabdrivers, right?"

"Right."

"Or dogs?"

"Dogs, too."

I turned onto his street, and tried to find an address on a house for a moment before I got one. Now I knew where he was.

"OK, I'm about thirty seconds out. Step out of the house and to the curb, right now."

"Yes, sir."

"Say thank you."

"Thank you, sir."

"And when I pull up, you are going to hand me a twenty dollar bill the moment I'm there, before you even get into the cab—the fare is about fifteen to downtown—and you are going to say, 'This should about cover it—keep the change,' OK?"

"Got it."

"And if I get even a hint of rudeness out of you, I'm going to leave your sorry ass and hers right in the middle of the fuckin' freeway, with cars going ninety on every side of your sorry self and hers and you're going to be really fucked then and if she's a smart girl it will be your last date for sure. Got it?"

"Got it."

I spied a couple on the street ahead, to the right. The taller of the two waved hesitatingly.

I smiled, hung up the phone, and headed toward them. 🔲

Lucky

Hey all you rich wives and girlfriends sitting around at home watching the kids while your businessmen husbands and boyfriends travel the world on their fat expense accounts you should know that after dinner your man just doesn't sit around his hotel room watching the weather channel or Fox News till bedtime when he is really out at the casinos dropping cash and hitting the strip clubs getting lap dances from supple young ladies that are a bit more intimate than you'd care to know about but while it might not seem so at first you are really lucky that you got a man with at least a bit of a conscience in that he isn't asking me to bring a hooker to his hotel room at the Hyatt like the keynote speaker at the conference on Homeland Security just did. ▣

William

Every morning, about 3:15 or so
William rides eastbound past the bus station,
on his big, red, balloon-tired Schwinn
that was new in 1964.

He always wears an oversized, blue, hooded
sweatshirt, and brown, leather hands
nearly the size of boxing gloves,
inflated with time and arthritis,
echoes of work performed long
ago, when the earth was young.

His legs drive slowly, but surely,
spinning around the bike sprocket,
in synchronous orbit with the ethereal music
that whispers through downtown if one
listens.

That time of the night
I often find myself parked
in the lot across from the bus
hoping for a flag from the 3:05
Greyhound out of Denver.

William always waves,
and sometimes when he sees it's me
waving back behind the wheel of the Yellow Cab

he rides over and I pop the trunk,
and we bungee cord his bike,
in the gaping maw of my giant trunk.

We roll out of the parking lot
and head to the Copper Lounge,
where William will spend the next six hours
swamping it out, for the minimum wage,
in preparation for the drunks of tomorrow.

It's only a five-buck run, but all uphill for
William's seventy-six-year-old legs (as of last July 4)
not that I am saying that they are weak,
as I suspect that they are as strong as his grip.

I never want him to pay for the ride,
because I like him and have nothing
better to do anyway,
but he insists.

I drive slowly for the conversation,
and William appears
to enjoy the comfort of my big backseat,
as he catches his breath.
Shallowly.

Both his boys have passed,
but his grandkids and great-grandkids
are doing fine, he says,

but he still has to work, because
the Social Security isn't enough
and the Medicare doesn't cover
the $237 a month
for his seventy-four-year-old wife's painkillers—
cancer you know,

We have our faith, too he says, *and every
day we thank the Lord
for giving his children
morphine.*

And William isn't one to complain,
as his grandparents were slaves in Alabama,
and he's quite pleased to be
a free man in Albuquerque
whatever his woes,
because as he tells me,

*all men have woes,
but not all are free.*

A Secret About Birds

I am going to tell you
a secret
that only the night people
know.

Day people think
that the birds waken
each morning before
dawn,
and begin to sing.

Night people know better.
We know
that the birds,
have been up
all night.

Whispering. ▣

The Life

He just didn't look right. Basketball player size, but hunched over. Maybe six feet seven inches or more, hard to tell. When he stepped off of the curb at the Nine-Mile Hill Flying J on the west edge of town, he stumbled, tottered, then caught himself and lurched toward my cab. He could have easily fallen, and I am not sure that he could have raised himself from the asphalt without help. He managed to fold himself into my cab like an origami bird brought to life.

"Clumsy, aren't I?" he laughed.

"I've seen worse," I said.

"I bet."

"Where you wanna go?"

"Walgreens, Coors and Central, and back. I've got a legal addiction and I've got a prescription to fill."

I put the cab in drive and backed away from the curb.

"Pharmacy?"

"No, the liquor department."

"Ah, who'd a guessed?" I said.

"Not many. And no one will ever know as long as you, me, and Johnny keep quiet."

"Johnny?"

"Johnny Walker Red," he laughed. "Come on brother, you never heard that one before?"

"Maybe, if so, I've forgotten."

He reached into his pocket and handed something to me.

"Here's a twenty now. That OK?"

"There's not a cabdriver I know that doesn't appreciate money up front."

"Now when we get there, you're going to wait for me, aren't you?"

"Sure. Don't worry about it."

"Another driver left me once."

"Well, that wasn't me, was it?"

"Not that I can remember, but it doesn't seem like you're the guy."

"I'm not. Don't worry, I won't leave you."

"Thanks. I'm not a rich man. The only money I have is the twenty that I gave you and the twenty that I'm going to use to buy me a bottle. And you know that I am not in good enough shape to walk back. Well, maybe I could and maybe I couldn't, but either way I'd worry about falling down and maybe hurting myself and me waking up with busted head and a coyote gnawing on my ears."

I thought about asking why a man would spend his last forty bucks on a taxi ride and a bottle, then realized that I already knew the answer.

I pulled up to the Walgreens, let him out, then backed into a space so I could watch the door. A habit. I liked watching the door. After a few minutes, I got out. Walked around the cab once. Stretched, arms up, tiptoes. Pulled my left arm to the right across my chest, twisted, and stretched. Then the other side, the same. Back up on tiptoes. Back down again. Did a few pushups against the hood. Walked over and admired a border collie in the bed of a pickup. Saw Amy the security guard come out of the building for a smoke, and wandered over to find out how her night was going. "Fine, no troubles," she said. "Only had to roust one shoplifter." I walked back to the cab, inspecting litter and the patterns of oil in the asphalt. I was leaning against the cab watching a bat taking out the moths flickering around a streetlight when my guy came out and tripped, almost dropping his bottle as it started to slip out of the paper sack that it had been wrapped in. Amazingly, he caught it, then did a stiff-legged Frankenstein-like trot to the cab.

"Sorry it took so long! They were training a new girl at the cash register!"

"That's OK, let's go."

I started the engine as he fell into the backseat, pulling in his legs with his hands, finally managing to shut the door, panting. The meter said $17 as I pulled out of the parking lot.

"Shit, that took so long the twenty isn't going to be enough."

"It'll be fine," I said. "I'm not going to make you walk and have to fend off coyotes."

"Oh, there *is* a God, thank you!"

"No problem."

I pulled onto Coors and headed for the interstate. It was more expensive that way, but faster, and since his twenty was gone, it didn't matter.

"Back to the Flying J?" I asked, as I pulled the steering wheel to the right to allow us to come off the interstate.

"No, just stop on the bridge over the highway. North end."

"Why there? That's the middle of nowhere." Well, maybe not quite, I thought, but there is nothing out there. And the Flying J is maybe half a mile away.

"Sure there's something there."

"What?"

"My home."

"There aren't any houses out there."

"Didn't say there were. But my home is."

I thought for a moment. Could there be a house, or even a shack there? No. There was absolutely nothing there, and I knew it.

"OK, I give up. Where is your home?"

"Under the bridge."

"You're kidding me."

"Nope, I live under the bridge."

"That must be tough . . ."

"Not at all. I have cardboard walls that I can put up or down depending on the season, a little rock-lined fireplace, an old mattress that fell off of a truck, a radio, and a little supply of canned goods. Want to come down and see? We can split the bottle if you want. Turn up the radio and tell lies to each other if you like?"

"No thanks," I said. "I've got to bring money home. Kids have to eat. And not that it's any of my business, but how do you get enough to eat way out here? We're miles from town."

"But not from the Flying J, and I'm a hard workin', enterprisin' man. Every morning I go over there and sweep up the lot, and the manager gives me breakfast. If a cook screws up an order, the girls will save it for me for later. Every once in a while a trucker will want his cab cleaned out and I'll do that for a couple of bucks. That's how I'll buy batteries for my radio, and pay for a taxi ride to Walgreens once a week to get my booze. They treat me real nice over there at the Flying J, sometimes even letting me watch TV in the trucker's lounge as long as no one minds. I do my laundry in a restroom sink, and there are showers for the truckers they let me use. And I come over here to sleep and relax. And way out here in the boonies there are no neighbors to complain to the cops that there is some bum over there sleeping under the bridge. Plus I like watching the traffic go by beneath me."

"Sounds like you have it pretty good," I said as I pulled to a stop at the north end of the bridge.

"Yes, sir, I sure do. Believe me, I don't think that I could have it any better. I live *the life*. For sure." 🖼

Boys on Bikes

Boys on bikes work the dark streets off East Central, hard,
like their fathers worked *rancheros* on horses,
chopped weeds in chile and corn fields with short-handled hoes,
waded in arsenic in silver and copper mines,
and swatted flies and dripped sweat, pig, chicken,
and cattle blood at slaughterhouses and *carnicerías*.

The boys flap at the streetlights like moths,
retreating to dim corners when headlights splash
across asphalt as slowly rotating tires crunch glass,
gravel, and cockroaches, as the cops cruise the streets haltingly,
hoping they might actually see something.

Streets greasy wet, rainwater puddled with crankcase oil,
blended by the monsoons of July.

Streets blasted and pockmarked by mountain after mountain
of windblown, eastbound sand,
salted with the yellow-brown cottonwood leaves of October.

Streets crisp and iced with the lurid, green, antifreeze frosting of January.

Streets blowing fog and plastic Wal-Mart bags with smiley faces
    in March,
mixed with assorted other trash—paper, plastic, and human.

Boys in caps, black stocking and baseball, the latter always turned
    backward for the
catchers they are, and the former looking senseless most seasons
    as if it matters.

Baggy shirts, shorts, sweats, tailored for cold, heat, wind, and rain,
  always secondhand but custom-designed for the smart boys
  they are.

Small bikes are best for teenage boys,
quick turns a must for stunts,
girls might be watching after all,
and if they aren't they still might have to *move*.
Twenty-one-inch wheels maybe, what we would have called a Sting-Ray
  bike with a banana seat when I was a kid just a century ago.

Because small bikes are best for boosting
over a wall
over a fence
or to toss to a shoulder for a sprint
across a vacant lot with broken bottles
and pieces of cinderblock some painted, some not,
should the need arise.

Boys on bikes swoop around my cab,
in and out, up and down, like kestrels riding warm thermals
looking for rabbits. Or mice. Or here, rats.

And when I slow down they glide in, and one pauses next to me
a professional courtesy,
while the others orbit, irregularly, in a pattern like flies tied to a filament
too small to see.

I toss a nod to the backseat, or a thumb over my shoulder
and they talk with the fare,
a scared businessman with a silk suit and an expense account, or
a gap-toothed trucker who didn't know how to score at the TA or
  Flying J, or

a middle-aged health-club-buffed husband with a skinny wife with no
    ass and a big unforgiving mouth out of town, or
a couple of scared frat boys clutching their crotches in the dark, or
a cracker who just drifted in to just drift out, or
some lowlife smartass shithead that somehow
found his way out of the world and into the blue bench seat of the
    back of my cab.

"Whatcha need, homes,"
the boys say, don't ask,
and the conversation rushes, like a glacier.
And I don't listen,
'cause I don't know anything,
it's just two guys talkin'
and it's none of my business,
except for what the meter says,
mo' better, mo' good.

And sometimes we follow the boys on bikes,
a block or two or eight,
to a tall, rangy man in sweats
and big-footed Nikes,
who emerges from behind a dumpster of the Circle K
or from behind a bush, or a parked car, or thin air,
but never from an apartment door,
or a house, we might remember,
sometimes the same man
sometimes not,
a tall, ghostly ghoul
always.

And we never see his face, under the hood,

maybe his chin,
when the deal is made
for rock, mostly rock,
or some mystery substance
in a plastic or paper bag,
that contains a ticket to
somewhere else.

Or sometimes it's a girl that's wanted,
and the mouth in the backseat makes its request;
a blonde, or Latina, or a black girl
from the smorgasbord of whores available.

And when the delivery is made,
the boys on bikes take their rake,
from the man with the hood,
and the girl, sometimes both,
these young entrepreneurs with a head for business.

And how sad it is, that they're working the street,
rather than pursuing one of the legitimate
employment opportunities open to them,
like being a dishwasher at Denny's,
or working the counter at Taco Bell,
or being a bag boy at the Wal-Mart

Supercenter.

Backloop

The backloop coming off
the port has a bit of a
roller coaster feel to it,
especially if one
accelerates
fast enough, slipping
out from under the canopy,
past security,
dipping into a loop
to the left,
then slowly rising
into a right hand
banked curve,
then loop to the left,
bank right,
then left,
climb,
then SOAR out
of the port and down
the deep dip
on Sunport
onto I-25.

When we come out
of the pop
and look down into the
Rio Grande Valley
below,
and see the volcanoes to
the west,

and the Sandias to the east,
or if it is night
and we see the splash
of city lights under
the Milky Way,
sometimes I can tell
by their reaction
if my fare
has never been
here before.

Sometimes I can tell
because of a change
in the quality of the air,
or perhaps the electricity
in their body changes,
or the humidity,
or pheromones,
I don't know.

But sometimes a
simple sigh gives them away,
or an exclamation of the beauty
of our little valley,
or a question
illustrates their
interest in the
city below.

And so with their cue,
I say,
ya wanna hear the spiel?
and if they say yes

(they always do)

I give it
to them. The spiel,
the same spiel,
over and over again,
and again,
and again.

So here it is,
more or less.

Below you is the Rio Grande
Valley, it's a great rift valley,
like the great rift valley of Africa,
where two continental plates meet,
and in the rift the river flows, from
its beginnings in the mountains
of Colorado to the Gulf of Mexico.

Those bumps on the horizon to
the west are volcanoes.
They last erupted
150,000 years ago.

To the east are the Sandias;
that means Watermelon, 'cause they
turn pink at sunset, and those are
the Manzanos, that means apple.
Don't know why they are called
that except maybe 'cause they are smaller
and pink too,
at sunset.

That hotel there is La Posada;
it means resting place in Spanish.
It was a Hilton once and it is
where Conrad Hilton
married Zsa Zsa Gabor.

The population is 448,606,
750,000 in the metro area,
under two million in the state,
making our city
smaller than Dublin,
or your city,
for sure.

Right about here is
where the famous Route 66
meets the El Camino Real,
the Royal Road from Mexico City
to Santa Fe,
so imagine the conquistadors
walking about

here.

And as for the economy,
there is tourism,
and we are proud of
our men and women
at Kirtland Air Force Base,
but the real business here
is government, capital G,
thanks to our national labs
and the bases

and the University.

And when we arrive
at their
destination,

I say,

Have a good time.
Welcome to the
Land of Enchantment,
please spend lots of money.

Then they laugh,
and pay me
and then I roll off
to the next fare,
and everyone is happy,
and the tourists feel that
they just met an authentic

taxi driver
in an exotic city,
and that they escaped,
unscathed,

and that they now have a
mental piece of the exotic, and soon
they will have a real chunk of it
when they buy a

trinket,

a pot,

a rug,
or some jewelry
in Old Town,

to prove
they were here,
to their friends
back home,

and display us
on their mantelpiece,
like a trophy head,

shot and stuffed
by the great hunter—
world traveler and
explorer of exotic realms.

Sometimes,
I have the urge
to give a different spiel,

something like:

*That is the Rio Grande
once a great river,
now a sewage ditch
that doesn't
even make it
to the ocean
anymore
we've bled it so.*

And those rocks

at the foot of the
volcanoes are
a sacred Indian
shrine of rock
carvings the rednecks
shoot at for target practice
and the mayor
is going to put a highway
through to a place
no one lives yet
so the developers
can make some money
selling land and building
shitty houses.
(And did I mention that
the mayor and
our great Senator Pete
own land
over there?)

And at the foot
of those Manzano
mountains there are
over two thousand nuclear
bombs, and over there
to the left
in about 1957
the Air Force dropped an
atom bomb on the south
end of town by accident,
and luckily
the triggering mechanism

wasn't set and when it fell
it only made a big hole in
the ground and a pilot
and bombardier
wet their pants.

And the rich people
that party at La Posada,
do you think that they
ever think of the
one out of ten New Mexican
children who will go to bed
hungry tonight
while they suck their
cocktails down?

And for that 750,000
people who live in the area,
that won't be the case for
long 'cause our aquifer
is going dry
in our lifetime,
yours and mine,
and this city will go the
way of Chaco
(look it up if you don't
already know).

And those conquistadors,
they marched right up the
valley and massacred
hundreds of Indians in
about twenty villages to the north,

near the Santa Ana Star Casino,
and their defenders
at the University today say that
the massacres were OK
because the Spanish
were better to the Indians
than the English were,
out east,
and besides, the Indians
have casinos now and are
economically empowered today
because the Spanish were so
good to them in the past.

And for that economy,
thank God for
Senator Pete,
tough-talkin'
fiscal conservative
out of the one side of his
mouth that lives in D.C.,
while out of the other
side of his mouth he brags
to us about bringing
back to New Mexico
over two bucks
worth of pork for
every buck we send
to Washington
in taxes.

And oh yeah,

isn't it amazing how
Old Town gets bigger every year,
and that the Indians that sit under the portal
and sell jewelry
don't really make the jewelry;
most just sell it as agents
for the galleries,
but buying from a real, live
Indian under a portal rather than
in a chic gallery makes for a more
"authentic" experience
for you, even though about
half of the jewelry you might buy
is really made in China?

And while I might
think I'll do this spiel
for a tourist or two,

I never do,

'cause I just might
not get

a tip,

and because no one
wants to know the truth
about our Land of Enchantment.

Even me,
on the backloop.

Wildlife

Being a cabdriver
gives one
lots of opportunities
to observe wildlife.

Like the mottled pigeons
circling a parking lot,
soaring, then diving,
in near synchronicity,
in response to silent
and mysterious commands,
their source
visual, vocal, or magnetic,
I'm not sure,
toward a few french fries spilling
out of a red cardboard carton.

And the dozen or so
rabbits, in holding,
near the Wyndham Airport,
chewing grass in relative peace.
Processing cellulose in
their two-chambered
stomachs, these
coprophagist leporids
are largely
untroubled

by the three-legged coyote
who lives nearby.
It appears that the coyote chases
the rabbits more
out of a genetic mandate
than anything else
because his dinner really
comes from the leftovers
cabdrivers leave in fast food
bags in trash cans,
or close to them anyway.

And the cooing
white-winged doves,
who have migrated
two hundred miles northward
of their historic range
in the past twenty years,
in response to the
warming earth,
that sit in the park
near the shop.

And Willie the rat,
and his family,
who hang out behind the
dumpster by the employees'
entrance to the Marriott
when I drop off Jeanette

to reconcile the books
at 4:30 a.m.

And then there are the
roadrunners, who
dance with a lizard in their mouth,
bent, like Groucho
smoking a lizard,
their tailfeathers splayed
like Groucho's coattails.

And then downtown,
at the club scene,
we have baying hounds
roaming in packs,
chasing pussy,
night after night
after night,
in response to silent
and mysterious commands,
their source
visual, vocal, or magnetic,
I'm not sure.

Good Bye

"Here you go, hon," said James, from my backseat. I was dropping him at his hotel on west Central, the Express Inn. A dump, but not the worst.

I looked at the crisp ten, barely visible in the light of the hotel neon sign, and folded it into the binder clip that holds my money. I did it in the open, something I rarely do. But James didn't care about my money. He was a regular, safe. A five-buck run and a five-buck tip.

"Thanks, and see you next time," I said.

"I don't think there will be a next time," he sighed.

"You getting a car? Moving?"

"Moving, dear. I've discovered that I am the oldest queer on the strip, and am having trouble dealing with it."

"Why is that?" I asked, popping the overhead light on, and turning in my seat. James always looked dapper. Tonight he wore black slacks with suspenders; a red bow tie topped his pleated crisp white shirt. Wrinkles radiated around his brown eyes, like petals on a sunflower.

"Oh, being the oldest queer is heartbreaking—as you can imagine. Yesterday I was young, witty, and pretty, and today I rarely draw a glance from anyone. And I am such an old-fashioned queer. I like a bit of bourbon and the aroma of pot now and then, but meth and crack—not my style. The scene here just isn't mine anymore."

"Where are you going?"

"Oh, some place where the bathhouses sparkle, where a young man might cast a favorable glance at an older man now and then, where the conversation is always pleasant yet challenging, and where there is a queer or two older than I."

"Good luck," I said.

"Thank you. I'll need it on this journey, eternally searching for the oldest queer in the world, until I discover, at long last, that it is I." 🁢

Whores

It was three in the morning of a year-long night when I made the mistake of catching her eye. Or more accurately, her eye caught me. It wasn't a big mistake, but like many mistakes, it wasn't recognizable immediately. She didn't wave, didn't hop into the street like some fares do, and she wasn't an open bid I won from dispatch. She simply looked at me from the street corner as I passed and her eye cast a net that snared me. She reeled in my Yellow Cab like a marlin, and drew me up on the curb like it was the deck of a trawler. The only thing missing was the pike in my gills. The place was east Central Avenue, not in the dangerous area we call the War Zone, but in a place that was worse. In the daytime the street looks fine. A Mexican fast food joint, a couple of dumpy hotels, a thrift shop or two, and a few bars. At night it's different. It's toxic. It's a human Superfund site where drug dealers and hookers ply their wares and the cops only pretend to care.

And most of it happens outside of Roberto's Mexican Food, open twenty-four hours. Roberto's is a white cinderblock A-frame with a cherry-red roof. The few people who actually go there for food use the drive-through, but if you're brave and visibly armed you can safely use the walkup. No tables, and supposedly no loitering. But there, perhaps because it is the only thing open all night for blocks, they hang, drawn like moths to a porchlight. Rumor is that the food's bad and the cockroaches as big as burritos. I've never eaten there, but have heard rumors of it happening. Occasionally, if a rude out-of-town fare wants fast food I'll take them there, hoping the karma train hits them with a digestive disorder.

She was new to the street—round and oily like a Greek olive just out of the jar—only pink. At fifty feet through a car windshield she had a pretty face.

She climbed in smelling like a high school boys' locker room. "Got some gum?" she asked. I handed her a stick of Doublemint, out of a pack left by fare a night or two ago. "Thanks," she said. "My husband hates it when I have dickbreath and it's not his dick."

"Understandable," I said.

"I'm only going to the Nob Hill Motel, just down the street." She pointed as if I might need instructions.

Damn, I thought, as I pulled back into traffic. Five bucks, tops.

"I've seen you before," she said. "What's your name, sweetie?"

"John," I lied.

"That's nice. My name is Henrietta. Glad to meet you."

"My pleasure," I said, knowing that a woman in the backseat of my cab who says that she is happy to meet me is likely to be as much trouble as a man who calls me bro. They all want something—probably a free ride.

"You look *strong*," she said, reaching out of the pit of the backseat to squeeze my shoulder.

"Thank you," I replied.

"And handsome too."

"That's what my wife says."

She laughed and slumped back in her seat. "Can't blame a girl for trying, can you?"

"Nah. Wives don't matter to a lot of men," I replied.

"Now ain't that the truth . . ."

We hit a red light that I should have avoided and I slowed to a stop, a bit too far into the intersection. The seconds ticked by. In the silence I thought I felt a few capillaries pop in my face and a few ghosts gather enough energy to become visible, or I thought they did anyway.

The light changed. I came alive and the ghosts scattered.

"I only have two dollars," she said.

I looked at the meter. It read $3.20 and we were only part of the way to her hotel.

"My husband took the twenty-five I had," she said. "Asshole."

So that is what she wanted, I thought. I wasn't pissed, as I'd rather have a hooker stiff me than have a short drop with a lawyer paying cash.

"You can have the two dollars," she said, "or a blow job." I looked into the rearview mirror. She smiled. She had all her teeth. A hand went to the top button of her dress and she started unbuttoning it. Slowly.

My eyes wandered back to the road, and I drove with the thought of a two-dollar blow job being oddly intriguing. I had never heard of such a thing. And the math was interesting. Could I buy ten for twenty bucks? Or, if I paid twenty bucks for one, would it be ten times better than a two-dollar one? I almost asked her how could a blow job be so bad that it could be worth only two bucks, but I didn't. Instead I drove the remaining blocks to the Nob Hill Motel, thinking about whores.

Ambar, a middle-aged bald cabdriver from India, had a theory about whores. The night he told me his theory it was dead slow.

No one was going anywhere, and he and I were sitting in holding, our cabs side by side.

We were watching a roadrunner chase lizards. Unlike the cartoon caricature, the brown, mottled birds are horizontal and purposive rather than vertical and speedy. They have wicked stiletto beaks and a punk crest. When you think rock star and roadrunner at the same time, think Sting. The object of our attention drilled a lizard, then looked at us. He was making a living, even though we weren't.

Ambar spoke. "You know, my friend, over the many years that I have been a cabdriver I have learned that there are two kinds of whores."

"Is that right?" I asked. "What are the two kinds?"

He smiled. "There are educated whores, and uneducated whores."

I thought about this for a moment, watching a plane approach from the west.

"How do you tell them apart?" I asked.

"With very, very, very much conscientious investigation and extensive personal interviews."

Beth worked the truck stop. She was a pretty girl—even after you knew what she did for a living. I wormed my way through the truckers and gas pumps and picked her up in front of the Duke City Diner. Open twenty-four hours. Lots of neon, chrome, and fifties memorabilia spiked by the smell of diesel fuel. And a green chile cheeseburger that would make a tourist scream. She wasn't dressed like a hooker. She wore blue jeans, snakeskin cowboy boots, and red tank top with a bra underneath. A back-pack hung over her shoulder. White girl, slim, nice ass, lots of dark brown, straight hair. She could have been a college girl.

"A good night?" I asked when she climbed in.

"Not bad," she said. "Eighty bucks an hour for about four hours. Were *you* ever that good?"

"Never. But my work's not worth that kind of money. Yours had better pay well—especially at a truck stop. One of those guys could drag you into the cab, knock you on the head, and have you across the state line before anyone knew what had happened."

"Nah, it's not that bad. I know most of the guys that I see, and most of the rest of them are just lonely. I've cut down on the ones I don't know though, and for the most part I just see a few boyfriends who pass through and give me a call on the cell on their way through town. Young guys, old guys, all of them OK though." Almost as an afterthought, she added, "I don't do the bad guys anymore."

I pointed my hood ornament toward the volcanoes and headed west on Menaul. She lived just this side of the river, past Old Town near where Mountain Road dead-ended. Lots of old adobes and trailers. A nice part of town. I wish I lived there. I didn't know exactly where she lived, as she was smart enough not to let cabdrivers or anyone else who knew she was a hooker know which house or apartment was hers. When we got into the neighborhood she got out and stood in the street watching us drive away. If she liked you, she waved. If she didn't, she just watched you pull away. She didn't walk to her house or apartment until we were long gone.

"My date tonight was an old guy—maybe fifty. I love the old

guys. They make you feel special. This trucker tonight reminds me of the councilman—treats me like a lady and has plenty of cash. He even brings me presents like the councilman does." She held up a teddy bear. "See?"

"You say a councilman is a client? Which one?"

"You know the fiscally conservative, socially liberal, tough-on-crime guy?"

"The guy on TV all the time? The guy that made it onto the TV show *COPS*?"

"Yep, that guy. He's married and a grandpa, you know. Takes his ring off when we fuck then crosses himself and asks the Lord for forgiveness afterwards. Makes him feel better, I guess. Danger isn't really a problem for me. Aside from the truckers, I date lots of professional guys. Businessmen, lawyers, teachers, you know, more than just your regular working guy. The professional guys can't date, let alone fuck, the office staff anymore without a lawsuit, so they get a quick BJ from a girl in the business when they need it. No complications since it's a professional deal. What I don't understand is the college guys. The sorority girls can't give it away fast enough and here the cute, little, dummy boys still pay me and the other girls for it."

She kept going, almost lecturing me. "And once you do those big shots once, they're yours as long as you're in the business, 'cause once you've had their dick in your mouth they know you're not some girl cop. And then they'll want you to fuck their buddy and their buddy's buddy. Damn lucrative. Speaking of referrals, if you get guys looking for a date tonight could you call me if I give you my number?"

"Sure, no problem," I said, knowing that I wouldn't.

"You know most of the guys I do are married? These married guys are the reason why I'll never get married. Nearly every married guy I know is fucking someone other than their wives, mostly me. You're married, right?"

"You know I am."

"So who are you sleeping with besides your wife?"

"No one."

"She special or something?"

"Sure."

"What? I'm not special?"

"Of course you are," I said. "I didn't mean it that way."

"You're a fucking liar," she laughed. "But a nice one. I forgot to say that all men are liars as well as cheaters and that's another reason not to get married." She turned coy. "How 'bout I crawl over the seat and give you a free one?"

"I'll think about it," I said, not wanting to be rude.

"All men cheat on their women eventually, and more than just in their minds, and so will you someday. Maybe with me."

I shrugged and concentrated on driving through Old Town past the museums. The sidewalks were filled with stumbling tourists carrying bags. Experience had taught me that the large bags were filled with cheap T-shirts and moccasins, lumpy bags with pottery, and small bags with jewelry. I eyed the tourists carefully—most were as oblivious to traffic as small children playing. I watched them closely because running over a tourist would ruin my day.

"Shit. Turn around," she said. "I'm going to party. I wasn't, but I have to go into rehab tomorrow, so I'm partying tonight. You want to party with me? That's my last invitation."

"No, but I'll drive you there," I said.

"Guess you're not the partying type. You're the money-making kind of taxi driver, not the whoring doper kind. Take me to the church in Martineztown. Please."

I looped through the plaza. Three lefts—Romero, South Plaza, then San Felipe—took me back to Mountain. People, mostly Indians, had jewelry laid out in front of them on blankets for the tourists to look at and hopefully buy. This was part of the authentic Old Town experience for tourists. This made them feel good, like being part of the Old West. They were also able to talk with real, live Indians for perhaps the first time in their lives, and even better, to give them money. Some kind of atonement for the white folks, I thought, and therapy at the same time. The tourists didn't know that most of the Indians selling jewelry didn't make the jewelry, and that most were actually salespeople for galleries and stores. They just knew that talking to the Indians made them feel good, buying from them better. It was almost as if they were buying a piece of the person to take home with them. It gave me the creeps.

"This is my fifth time for rehab. I hope it takes this time. I've got to get off the street before I wind up like Glenda."

"Who's Glenda?"

"Glenda's a girl at the Fina, been there forever, has AIDS and about three teeth left. She never leaves and probably hasn't had a bath or shower in a year."

"And guys pay her?"

"A few. Enough that she can eat out of the vending machines every day and buy her smokes."

"If you and she are doing the same drivers, aren't you worried about AIDS?"

"We don't do the same drivers—my guys are high class. Besides, I use condoms like other people use Kleenex."

"What are you going to rehab for?"

"Heroin. I fucking hate it. Well, love it and hate it really. I love the high, but hate the life. I wouldn't be a hooker if it weren't for heroin. So, I have to kick it."

She paused. "You want to know what got me started on heroin?"

I nodded, turning left onto Broadway.

"I tried it once at a party when I was drunk and that was all it took. Just one time for me. Guess I'm weak. From party gal to hooker in about six weeks. Some cute philosophy-major dude told me it was fun, just another life experience, and that just doing it once wouldn't hook you."

"Think rehab's going to work?"

"Maybe. My heart's in it this time. I gotta get out of this—I'm twenty-eight, you know."

"No, I didn't. You look younger."

Her eyes caught mine in the rearview. She spoke in a soft voice. "No way."

"Really. Just like a college girl."

"I *was* a college girl. I was gonna be an accountant. Two years of school done. UNM. Now I just fuck like an accountant fucks. Maybe I'll go back to school once I shake this nasty shit."

I couldn't resist. "How does an accountant fuck?"

"How else? By the numbers man, by the numbers."

We exchanged smiles in the rearview as I pulled up to the old church in Martineztown.

"One house past the church, no, another. Here." The sun was

setting over the volcanoes, and in the distance the Sandias were turning pink, earning their name.

I looked at the church, one of the oldest in town. Simple, dignified, adobe. Something tourists once took pictures of, but a tourist hadn't been down this street in years. One oversize, white, wooden steeple reaching toward God as if he actually might pay attention. The churchyard was dirt, the neighbor's yards were dirt, dirt was everywhere. But it was well-lit, pretty dirt in the New Mexican light. The scene would fit an Adams photograph or an O'Keeffe painting. The only problem with the scene was the crack house next door to the church. But at least you had to walk in. Not very convenient. I knew a crack house near Pennsylvania and Central where you put money in a mailbox, honked, then drove around the block. When you came back, your crack was in the mailbox.

I pulled to a stop right out front. She opened the door behind me and slammed it shut in the same movement. "Be right back," she said.

I stopped her before she got too far. "Hey, why don't you forget the party tonight? Leave that shit alone. I'll take you home."

She waved me off.

"A free ride," I added.

She laughed. "You give free ones too? You're very kind, but we're here and now I'm in the mood. Besides, free ones really are never free, hon, you know that."

She walked into an old adobe house south of the church. I studied it for a moment. The adobe was crumbling near the ground and needed replastering. The swamp cooler wasn't hooked up even in this heat. No women here, I thought. Any decent New Mexican woman would have had a man at those tasks long ago or done it herself. A glance around the yard confirmed it. No toys. I hauled my stove-up body out of the cab, appreciative of the break and opportunity to stretch, especially with the meter running.

I stopped looking around, having forgotten that I probably didn't want to draw attention to myself, given that I was in the middle of a drug deal. I leaned against the fender. If I smoked, I would have lit one. I stared off at the skyline downtown, wondering where the people staying at the Hyatt got their drugs.

An old Hispanic man in a Dallas Cowboys baseball cap, dirty work pants, and a dirtier T-shirt left the house across the street and walked to the cab. He looked as if he hadn't shaved in two or three weeks, and his gray beard reminded me of a hedgehog. I'd seen him around and didn't like him.

"Eh, *carnal*, *es* she your girlfren?"

"No, why, you jealous?"

"*Claro, señor.* Any man no have pussy is jealous of man with pussy. *Especialmente un hombre viejo*, old, like me."

"So, you are an old man. Big deal. Find an old lady."

"*Tengo una viejita que no me quieres.* I have an old woman, but she no like me. She cook and clean sometimes but no fook."

"Try taking a bath. You're dirty and you stink."

He shrugged. "I did that once. No help."

He looked toward the house Beth had gone into with longing.

"Think this girl be my girlfren? I have plenty money."

"*No. Es impossible.* When we drove up she pointed at you and said that is one ugly old man. *Feo*, even for an old man."

"Que lástima. Oh, well. When the next time you fook her will you think of me?"

"Sorry man, I don't fook her and I wouldn't think of you if I did, you piece of shit *cabrón.* She is a lady on an errand, you dirty old goat, get out of here."

I reached for a rock like I would have had a barking dog been bothering me. I faked a throw and he limped back across the street to where he came from. He would have tucked his tail beneath him if he had one. I dropped the rock and when I turned around she was behind me.

"What was that all about?"

"He thinks you're cute, but I told him you're not interested."

"Wouldn't happen. He's a fucking *pendejo,"* she said climbing into the car. "This whore has *some* standards."

We headed back down Mountain, making small talk. She was distracted, rattling a paper sack. Looking in it, closing it, then looking into it again. The spell broke and then she dug into her wallet. Two twenties floated over my shoulder, dropping like flower petals onto the seat beside me.

"You know, I put in my application at Lindy's on Central yesterday," she said, as we pulled up to her stop and her door opened.

"Good for you. Good tips there, maybe. Pretty girls always get good tips."

She climbed out of the cab, closing the door gently.

"Bye, hon," she said through the open window.

"Next time," I said.

"I really was a college girl—just a few years ago."

"Work hard at rehab and maybe you will be again."

"I really want to be an accountant."

"Well, if you make it, I'll hire you."

"You would?"

"Sure, everyone needs an accountant to help them cheat on their taxes," I said, pulling away from the curb. The cab kicked a little gravel as I pulled away.

I looked in the rearview. She clutched her paper sack and waved.

■

Banana-nose Julie waved me over at Pennsylvania and Central, and I pulled into the Circle K. She ran over to the cab as I rolled down the window. Her boobs bounced under her red tank top as she ran, and a couple of guys in a car driving by shouted approval.

"You seen Maxine?" she said gently, her southern upbringing clear. Her makeup ran down her cheeks.

"Not tonight. What's wrong?"

"She climbed into a gray Lexus two nights ago with two or three guys in it, and the next thing I know her head is bobbing up and down in the backseat and everything seemed fine—normal and all, and they drive away all regular-like. I thought everything was OK, but they never brought her back and her clothes and shit are still at my place."

"You tell the cops?"

"Yeah, but those assholes don't care. I told them she was missin' but when they found out that I didn't know her real name and didn't have a photo of her and when I said that she worked the streets they said that they couldn't do nothin'. I even got all dressed up and all in a nice white blouse and skirt and went to the cop substation way down the street at the 7-Eleven so they might not know I was a hooker and talked to them there and they still didn't do nothin'."

"I'll watch for her. And you've got to get off the street, girl. It could happen to you, too."

I handed her a tissue. She patted at her makeup with it then stashed it in her pants pocket.

"Shit, I don't know what to do," she said, starting to shake. "They say the Lord moves in mysterious ways and all, but he made me a whore and that's all I can say about that. But Maxine is a nice girl, she wasn't born a whore like me—she's just a fun-lovin' nineteen-year-old that didn't do no good in school or whenever she had people bossin' her around at work or anywhere."

Her hands moved to her hair, and she started tugging at it.

"The Lord just can't let anything happen to Maxine.

"He won't, will he?

"Will he?"

The guy patted Marvella's thigh tenderly, then climbed out of the cab and into the lobby of the Howard Johnson's on East Central.

"Thanks for stopping for me, sweetie, it's been a slow night."

"No problem. You're the prettiest girl out here tonight, and any night. All the guys want you when they see you."

And that was the truth. Marvella was model-lovely with an athlete's body and a face that belonged on *Vogue*, not on East Central. Unfortunately, an eight-year prison term for killing a man who had beaten her when she was eighteen put an end to most careers for her. She was one of the few girls who worked the streets who weren't into drugs, and actually put money away. She was also smart, working the bars downtown—not as a hooker looking for Johns but as just another young woman looking for a man with money that might be interested in something permanent. And the man she caught would never know about her past.

She touched my shoulder. "You're sweet. Now tell me about him."

"Not much to say. I picked him up at the Marriott, but I had to go in and have them call his room, so he's staying there, and has money. Said he thought he might like to drive around for a while and gave me a hundred-dollar bill. I figured that I knew what he wanted so I ran him up to Tramway and down to the University and back a couple of times and he didn't complain. We saw a few girls and he asked me if they were working girls, and I said who knows, but we can stop and ask if he wants, but he said no, let's find a black girl, and so I was happy running up the meter till he saw you. He says he's a stockbroker from Phoenix, that his wife is a bitch, and that he just liked to have a little fun when he was out of town like the next guy. Says he can't wait to get enough money so he can retire because stockbrokers don't help people anymore because they can't really study the stocks and make good recommendations, they just have to sell what stocks the upper management of the company wants them to sell, and that the whole economy is all a big conspiracy. Said he played football for Ohio State in the eighties and loved Woody Hayes. Actually, he looks sort of like Woody Hayes did when he was young."

"So, he doesn't sound like a cop?"

"No, he knows too much about something besides the street to be a cop."

"Think he's safe?"

"You know I can't tell you that that for sure."

The lobby door of the Howard Johnson's opened, and Woody Hayes walked toward us, grinning, key in hand.

Marvella sighed.

"Well, if he's not OK, I'll just have to fuck him up."

"Try not to kill him."

"OK, hon, see you later," she said, closing the door behind her.

"You just drove by it," said a voice behind me.

I looked around, put on the brakes, and remembered I had a fare. A whore. Taking her to the Nob Hill Motel. I turned around and pulled in, rocking to a stop.

"So, you want the blowjob, or the two bucks?" she said sweetly, looking out toward the street.

I stopped the meter. It read $5.20. I briefly thought about her peculiar proposal. I knew I didn't want either, but for a moment I didn't want her flagging down any more cabs without money. Then I realized that I didn't care about any of it, and that all of the whores I knew had certainly earned more than a few free cab rides.

"Keep them both," I said, finally. "Use the two bucks to buy some gum."

"I could sure use the gum," she said, laughing as she climbed out of the cab.

Hollywood

I'm sure that you have seen all of the taxi shows
on television.

Maybe my favorite is *Taxi*, with its all-star cast,
so stunning that I just have to name them all:
Jeff Conaway, Tony Danza, Danny DeVito,
Marilu Henner, Judd Hirsch, Carol Kane,
Andy Kaufman, and Christopher Lloyd.

While a good show, the critic in me says that
the characters spend way too much time talking
at the shop to make a good living and that real
taxi drivers are out in the world chasing money
and that if you think about it *Taxi* was a lot like
The Golden Girls except the setting was a cab shop
and Estelle Getty wasn't in a cage like DeVito.

And my lovely wife Annie says that as of the
fall 2002 season there is a television show on
Friday nights called *Hack* that I have never
watched because like David Morse, the driver in
that show, I spend Friday nights in my cab as well.

But she says he spends a lot of time out of his
cab running up and down alleys getting clubbed
and beating up people and talking with cops and
solving crimes and seems largely unconcerned

with cash flow, which is not realistic and apparently
he uses his taxi like a giant yellow duck blind so he
can drive anywhere he wants without the ducks being
bothered which is interesting but a bit contrived.

And then there is that fare favorite, *Taxicab Confessions,*
a show on HBO that all the young people apparently
watch, especially the drunk, cute girls who always ask
me "Are we on *Taxicab Confessions?*" then laugh to let
the guy that they just picked up at the club know that
they are ready for a tumble. And that show I have seen a
couple of times when the night drove me home early and
all I can say is that even stranger things happen in my cab
which might explain why every other episode of *COPS*
is filmed here in Albuquerque and that the drivers on
Taxicab Confessions are much homelier and dumber
than the homeliest and dumbest cabdriver in Albuquerque.

Which makes me think that Hollywood needs some
six-figure script consultants who know real cab action
and dialogue as well as the vicissitudes of modern life to
bring a touch of realism to their shows and I just happen
to know a guy who just might be able to make that happen
should some important producer with a fat wallet take notice.

I could even bring along a couple of my buddies. ▦

Volcanoes

Sitting in holding
waiting for the port
to move,

I stare toward the west mesa,
and at the half-dozen or so silent volcanoes
hunched on the horizon,
like old men gathered around tables
in a city park,
round-shouldered and grim,
nestled over checker games,
concentrating.

Oblivious to the
children playing
at their feet. ▣

Too Fast

I was
driving way too fast,
in the cradle of dawn,
when a dusky, gray streak
sliced across my
windshield and
thudded
into my bumper,
pinwheeling
across the street
and into someone's
lamb's ears and
wild mustard,
and I realized
that I had killed
a cat.

A young blond
woman,
still almost a
girl,
knelt over
the lifeless form,
tears flowing down
her round cheeks,
watering the miniature
flowers
on her nightgown.

From across the street
a slender man in khaki
shorts, a T-shirt the same
color as the cat,
and open-heeled,
green slippers,
ran
toward us.

He touched her velvet
fur, saw her slack
pink tongue,
and felt the
blood already beginning
to thicken under her,
her trauma hidden
from sight.

Unbuckling the collar,
its tag tinkling one last
time,
the man wrapped her in
a frayed blue towel,
like bunting,
tucked under the
chin of a newborn,
and retreated.

I pulled a garden hose
from the girl's yard,
and washed the red
blood off my Yellow
Cab, and from the street,
and from the lamb's ears
and mustard,
scrubbing,
till all was clean,
mostly.

I watched the water,
the blood, and the
girl's tears
swirl down the street
and into the gutter,
beginning their
journey to
the Rio Grande
below.

Seeing the
water, the
first spring robin
I had seen this year,
dropped down from
a mulberry tree,
alighted on the asphalt,
and took a drink.

Plenty of Places

The day drivers
are grumbling
because the city
cut down all
of the chamisa
in the back of holding,
behind the
Wyndham Hotel
at the Airport.

The night drivers
are unconcerned
because in the dark,
there are
plenty of places
in the city
to pee,
and bushes
need not
be involved. 🔲

Valentine's Day

I

Pepper, the stripper
who works at TD's,
made breakfast for her husband
on Valentine's Day, and first
learned something was wrong
when he threw it back at her,
eggs, toast,
potatoes,
plate, and all
and called her an ugly
whore.

Am I ugly? she asked,
from my backseat.
No, you're lovely, dear.
Am I a whore?
Hardly.

Her makeup ran teary,
ashen rivers
down her cheeks and chin,
as she convulsed and moaned
over lost love,
knees curled to
her chest, lying down
in my backseat,
rocking my cab,
like a fat man was

jumping up and down
on the trunk.

I took a sweaty
hundred-dollar bill she
stuffed in my fist
into the Phillips 66 at Coors
and Paseo del Norte
and bought her a pint
of Crown Royal
and a pack of menthol
Kools.

A spark of light, then
the smell of sulfur,
then menthol
and burning tobacco leaf
and something much like
death but not quite
filled the cab.

Then sweet smelling
Crown Royal,
the rushing over rocks
sound of
gurgling,
then the crash
of swallowing,
again and again,
waves slamming
against the shore
of her throat.

Drive, please,
she said, wiping her
mouth with the back of
her slender wrist,
back and forth,
almost violently,
grinding bone
against painted red
lips.

Maybe I can find him,
I think I know where
his girlfriend lives,
and if I find him there,
I'll fuck him up
bad.

Not a good idea, I said, gently,
with images of tortured angry
faces including hers, screaming,
flesh being pounded,
blood erupting from small
amateur-induced body traumas
pulsing through my mind,
and me in the middle
of a domestic,
one more time.

But his fucking girlfriend
didn't do nothing to me,
and I wouldn't want to ruin
her Valentine's Day,

even if it is with him.

So just drive.
Drive till the money's gone.

And so I drove. Fast,
my meter eating the hundred
at two dollars a mile, the quicker
the better, so I could let her off,
hopefully to make a hundred more
off someone else,
or maybe a dozen someones,
but first I had to rid myself of
the bag of tears now on the
floor of my backseat,
then climbing back
up,
hitting me on the shoulder,
not gently.

You men.
I hate you men.
We bleed, and bleed, and fucking
bleed ourselves to death
giving you babies.
And you don't fucking care.
I gave him our nine-month-old
daughter.
Our lovely daughter,
I coulda died.

We both coulda died,

my little girl and me.

And now I am nothing,
an ugly old whore.
And our little girl's daddy
betrayed her.
And me.

And you fucking men
don't think that
you're betraying the kids,
just us ugly old whores,
but you are,

the kids most of all,
she screamed.

So fuck Valentine's Day,
that little bastard Cupid,
he doesn't shoot an arrow,
he tosses a hand grenade
your general direction
and stupid bitches like me
run as fast as we can
to throw ourselves on it.

II

A giant khaki coat walked toward me out of the darkness,
its immense padding reminding me of an overinflated rubber life raft
with a plethora of pockets, perhaps filled with gear that
survivors of a shipwreck might find useful;
rations, flares, knives, fish hooks, and a compass
maybe.
For effect or function I am not sure, the coat was rigged with draw-
strings
    strung from
pockets, seams, and eyelets, as if the person inside could be quickly
    secured
to a fire hydrant or car bumper if the earth started to heave in some
    planet-rocking
cosmic wave of energy.

Then the coat's front doors opened and a woman disembarked
from its folds like she was walking down the gangplank of a ship,
not a mere life raft,
and she came ashore at the door of my cab
and found her way inside,
even without the compass.

You know a big black driver named Manny?
she asked from the backseat
in a thick Texas drawl
on our thirty-five-dollar run to the Double R.

I nodded, thinking of a big, brown, leather-wrapped
boulder of a man called Manny.

She shook her pretty, black hair,
smiled, and said,

Manny and I go way back,
he's my driver, my very own driver,
it seems at times,
and I love to talk to the big man,
and we talk about life, love, and how
good it would be for me to get my shit together,
someday.

And he preaches to me,
the word of God,
Jesus Christ our Lord,
and between the two,
the Lord and Manny that is,
they help me find my path,
and that sweet old boy Manny helps me with my sons,
with advice and shit,
and he tries to tell me when a man is no good,
just like the one who just dumped me
on the street,
back there,

and I try to listen, and it doesn't
always take,
but Manny forgives me,
when it seems no one else will.

So when you see Manny next time,
just tell him Linda loves him
and prays for him,
and between you and me, honey?
Just between you and me?

I nodded and she sighed.

Right now I'm praying that
someday, someday,
by God someday,
that big man Manny,
that big wonderful man
Manny,
will be my Valentine,
mine and mine alone,
instead of the piece a shit
Valentines
I always seem to have,
about February time.

And in the morning when we cashed in,
I said to Manny,
"Manny, I met a friend of yours,
pretty girl named Linda from the
Double R, who says you go way back,
and that she loves you,
and that she prays for you,
and thanks you for your help with her sons,
and your preaching her the word of God,
and helping her find a better path."

And big ol' Manny takes off his blue
baseball cap, scratches his head,
and says,

Whatchoo talkin' bout,
don't know no lady from the

Double R named Linda.

She says you do.

Was she nice?

Yeah.

Was she pretty?

Yeah.

I'd remember a nice girl from the
Double R.

I'd remember a pretty girl from the
Double R. You betcha.

She must have me confused with another
big black man who drives
a cab in this life or in another
she lives.

And he rolls back his
big round basketball of a head
and laughs.

And ain't that the shits,
pretty girl likes me and she
in another man's cab,
on Valentine Day,
and I don't know who
the fuck she is.

Story'a my life.

III

I had a Valentine once,
a lovely man, a gracious little
man with a ducktail haircut
back in 1957.

A man who used to roll his cigarettes
into the sleeve of his short-sleeved, white T-shirt
like they did back then,

said Myrtle, the nice lady at Circle K
in Midtown, as she took the $26.75
gas money from my hand,
and gave me my receipt.

And then when I wasn't looking,
my lovely little Valentine
somehow turned into
a deadbeat ex-husband
who wouldn't pay his child support,
the goddam lying dog,
and I've always puzzled since then,
if men just eventually turn into dogs,
like fruit rots with time,
or if they were born that way,
born as dogs,
and that it just takes a woman
a while to figure it out.

IV

Bill and Rudy,
the dumb asses I pick up
at Fantasy World,
the all-nude review,
complain when I ask
for money up front.

And I say it's nothing personal,
it's just a bias I have against everyone
who lives in their neighborhood,
which they accept.
And Rudy sighs and says,
we must be the only fuckin' guys
in the world tonight who are not getting laid
given it's Valentine's Day and all.
How the fuck can that happen,
how can we be so fuckin' lame?
All the free pussy in the world,
and we can't find any.
Everyone has a Valentine but us,
and I don't fuckin' believe it.

"The problem with you guys," I say,
"is that you've been looking for pussy,
when you shoulda been looking for a Valentine."

V

In the alley behind the Pulse,
two men kiss, and
one man rubs his hand,
lightly,
over the other man's
tight belly,
as I roll by, and my lights
flash on them,
then they turn shy,
and tenderly turn away,
from me,
but not each other,
as they move deeper
into the bushes,
on Valentine's Day.

VI

And so about midnight,
I tell Beverly,
a ghost of an old lady
and a regular,
who retired about a lifetime
ago, when I pick her up at
the nursing home and
take her to Sandia Casino,
that broken and bleeding
hearts
line the streets
of Albuquerque,
and maybe the world,
on Valentine's Day,
like armadillo roadkill
on a Texas highway
on Saturday night.

Ah, says Beverly,
Isn't love grand?
What I wouldn't give,
to be able to
break another
heart,
or two,
before I die.

Starry, Starry Night

Planes were landing like flies on a frosted donut. Thank God, my cab was at the port, Albuquerque Sunport that is, not hustling for flags on the street or chasing bad addresses or drunks. I was first island, which meant that I was first cab up, and after a long, dry spell, fares were pouring out of the terminal doors like July monsoon rain down a tight downspout. Leaning against my cab, I looked at their eyes, watching for those people who had that "get me outahere I need a cab" look. They were my ticket out of here as well. Most people blew by me, tired, grumpy, and heading for the parking garage. By their steady pace and the fact they never looked around I could tell they were locals with wheels. If they came out slow, craning their necks first left toward the terminal entrance, then right, they were locals with a ride. They just hadn't found it yet. Motherfathersisterbrotherhusbandwifefriendorlover either hadn't arrived, or were circling the terminal in a post-9/11 paranoia that didn't allow citizens to stop unless they were loading.

Then I saw them, my ticket out of here. Two slight figures in black washed up by the tide behind my open trunk. They were not looking at me, but they were. Well, their eyes didn't show it, their faces were looking almost at the ground, but their bodies faced me. I moved a little to the left. Their bodies shifted slightly. I moved to the right. Their bodies shifted again. Finally, the smaller of the two figures caught my eye, and I may have imagined a smile. Two ladies. Japanese maybe. Expensive, tailored cloth jackets, sensible, black flats. Young and younger. One small Gucci bag with handle and wheels heeling like a trained dog. I started for their luggage. Half a step away from my cab, I heard a thunk behind me. I turned and saw a salesman's display case sitting in my trunk with a salesman's hand still attached. He let it go, and dropped a garment bag on top. Sears. His ratty brown hair was a comb-over, his gray sportsjacket tweed and a size too small. Cheap, blue slacks, wingtips, and a tie from another millennium completed his attire. Smoke curled from an unfiltered cigarette held in a claw he would have called a hand.

"Ready to go, pal?" he croaked.

"Sorry sir, but this cab is for these ladies," I replied. I turned and was pleasantly surprised that they had closed the distance and their bags were nearly within arm's length. I snagged the bags, slipped them gently into the trunk on both sides of the salesman's gear. In one quick motion the salesman's luggage was resting on the curb.

"But I was here first," he said. I felt, but didn't see, the ladies grow tense.

"Sorry sir, but eye contact has priority over proximity, and these ladies made first eye contact," I said, bullshitting.

He took a drag off his cigarette.

"OK," he said. "And ladies first, anyway."

I opened the rear door, and my two fares climbed in smiling and nodding thanks to the gentleman. I closed the door, slammed the trunk, and walked swiftly around the cab. I popped the meter with my thumb. It was ticking before my butt hit the driver's seat.

"Where would you like to go this evening?" I asked.

"Santa Fe," said the eldest.

My heart skipped a beat. Bingo! I'm the man. Seventy-eight dollars and sixty-six cents and with a decent tip I would make my lease on the cab with one fare.

"Yes, ma'am. My pleasure."

I pushed the pedal, looked left to make sure I was clear, and keyed the mike.

"Two forty-six," I said

"Two forty-six," replied Butch the dispatcher.

"Two forty-six is Northbound. Santa Fe."

"Yippy kie yay!" said Butch. "Two forty-six is northbound. Have a safe trip."

I looped out of the terminal, leaving the concrete and metal structure for the asphalt of Sunport Boulevard. At the top of the loop as we exit, first-timers are often startled by the vista of the city below. Downtown sits below the airport, and the view of the city at night is breathtaking. A few tall buildings punctuate the valley below, and the long, dark ribbon of the Rio Grande splits the landscape horizontally. The view stretches for probably forty miles, and the cluster of lights at the heart of the city fades to the north and south. My fares were talking to each other in a language that sounded Japanese, but could have been Chinese, Korean, or a dozen other languages. All I knew was it wasn't Navajo. I braked and hit I-25 northbound oozing through traffic and the lights of the city, past SUVs, low riders, and trucks from the rez coming to town on a Saturday night.

We pierced the night, northbound, tires chewing asphalt. Two ladies from the Orient and I. As we passed the glow of Sandia Casino, I turned the radio off, the radar detector volume up, set the cruise control to eighty-one, and slumped in my seat, my bones turning into cabdriver rubber. If I focused I could be back for bar rush. Damn, I knew I should have stopped for coffee before I went to the port, I thought.

Just the other side of Algodones we escaped the envelope of luminescence that surrounds Albuquerque. The women chatted excitedly behind me, obviously tourists in New Mexico for the very first time.

Then the tone of their voices changed. Excitement and curiosity took a concerned, then frightened turn.

"Excuse me, sir, but something is very wrong!" said the woman behind me.

"I'm sorry," I replied, "What's wrong?" I feared that I had left a piece of luggage on the curb, or that they really hadn't wanted to go to Santa Fe, after all.

"The sky! The sky! Something is very wrong!"

I looked out the window and saw a beautiful New Mexican night. Stars strewn brilliantly, the Milky Way by Jackson Pollock.

"What, you see an airplane go down or something?" I said, slowing down and rolling down my window. The sound of the whine of my tires on the road and the smell of the desert at night blew in.

"No, the stars, the stars, something is very wrong with the stars!" The two women were now huddled in the backseat, the older one with her arms around the younger.

"What's wrong with the stars?" I kept looking up and around, seeing nothing new, a bit anxious about holding my cab to the road.

"Are you blind?" said the older woman. "They are so very bright! Something must be wrong with the earth's atmosphere! The stars look like this only from outer space! We must be witnessing some terrible natural disaster!"

I looked out the window again. "Well, I don't know about

where you ladies come from, but they look like this almost every night here. Believe me, it's not the end of the world."

They looked at each other, disbelieving. Finally, they started laughing, and the younger one spoke. "We come from Tokyo, and the most stars you will see on any night is two or three!"

"Well then," I said, "this is what the sky really looks like from Earth, and you ladies need to get out of Tokyo more often."

"Certainly, sir, you are right," said the younger woman. "Would you mind taking us off the main road so we can admire the stars?"

And so somewhere north and east of Santo Domingo I turned on the meter and pulled off the interstate. I drove down a gravel road until no artificial light could be seen. Not from a streetlight, a house, or a car. No lights, anywhere. When the night sky was as big as it ever gets, I stopped and shut off the engine. I climbed out, leaned against the cab, and then decided to take advantage of the break to stretch a little bit, and wandered up the road to give them some privacy. It would have been a good time for a smoke, if I smoked. Fifty yards away or so I looked back and saw them pointing at the sky. Sound carried, and their voices reminded me of what I imagine nestling hummingbirds sound like. I smiled when I thought of the meter ticking away.

Maybe someone on earth was happier and more content than those two ladies from Japan were at that moment, but I doubt it. They must have walked arm in arm for an hour. Finally, they indicated to me that they were ready to move on to Santa Fe by walking back toward the car. I moved to join them.

And then a coyote howled. 🖾

Afterword

As you know by now, I'm a cabdriver. I didn't know it at the time, but I became a cabdriver in the emergency room of Lovelace Hospital in Albuquerque, New Mexico, one warm, sunny winter afternoon in February 2001. A few hours before, my wife Annie, pregnant with our son Asa, had fainted at work. She had collapsed in the middle of teaching a class, and a friend had driven her to the emergency room. A few phone calls later, and between my classes (at the time I taught anthropology at the University of New Mexico) a student had found me and told me the news, so I hurried to the hospital.

There I received the wonderful news that she and Asa were fine, but that she shouldn't work anymore during the pregnancy. It didn't take us long to have a discussion that neither of us looked forward to—a conversation about the fact that without her working we would not be able to pay our bills. Like most Americans, we were a two-income family and needed two incomes to make ends meet.

But what could we do to pay the bills? Annie needed to focus on the pregnancy. She certainly couldn't work. That left me as the one who was going to have to come up with extra money. But I had no idea how. I am a teacher, a writer, and a researcher. That is what I know how to do. A small and very lucky minority of my colleagues have fat consultancies or trust funds, but like the vast majority of professors, I don't. And like teachers everywhere in the country, most professors at UNM don't make a lot of money. And so, like every other American who needs a second job, I nervously scanned the newspaper ads. What I needed was something part-time, with flexible hours, that paid reasonably well, that wasn't mind numbing, and hopefully involved no heavy lifting. In other words, the same job that everyone on earth wants.

That night I scanned the newspaper to see what opportunities might come my way. No job seemed as if it might work. Everything that I might be qualified for required a full-time commitment. Day after day I read the ads with growing desperation. Finally I saw an ad for a part-time opening in a bookstore. I was elated. I knew books if I knew anything. My life was, in many ways, devoted to books. I read nonfiction from many fields voraciously at work, and at home at night and on most weekends I read fiction. Every Sunday I devoured the *New York Times Book Review* to plan future reading. Pleased with the opportunity, I enthusiastically drove to the bookstore that was hiring, filled out the application, and waited for a phone call asking me to come in for an interview. And waited. And waited. The call never came. And I couldn't come up with the courage to call and ask why. It was depressing. I couldn't even get a job at a bookstore. With each passing day my concern grew. Bills were due soon and while I knew we could pay them this month, next month was another story. Everyone who has ever had to worry about how to feed and house a family knows exactly the sinking that I felt in my heart. While I grew more desperate with every passing day, Annie seemed calm. It almost seemed as if she knew that things would work out.

Finally, one chilly, star-lit, New Mexican winter evening, I took a long walk through our airport-area neighborhood. It was late enough that traffic had thinned, and the night was nearly still as I walked amidst the aroma of burning piñon spilling from my neighbors' fireplaces. Hands in my pockets, I stopped at a corner on Yale Boulevard and watched a car approach before I crossed the street. The headlights grew closer quickly, and it was clear that the car was speeding past me toward the airport remarkably fast. As it passed, I managed to see the color of the car and to read the sign on the side. *Yellow Cab.* Something clicked. "Hey, I can do that!" I thought. I walked home, my stride lengthening with every step. I opened the door, grabbed the evening newspaper and opened it up to the classifieds. There it was. An ad that had been there all along. It read, "Be your own boss. Part-time—flexible. Drive a Yellow Cab." The idea of driving a cab intrigued me. I am, after all, an anthropologist. It could be interesting. I would meet lots of people, drive around town, and move some luggage. Big deal. If only it paid enough (it did—but I can't tell you how much—to do so would violate the cabdriver code of ethics). So I applied. Much to my surprise, after a quick interview, a one-evening training session, and plunking down $35 to the city of Albuquerque for a business license, I was a cabdriver. To be specific, I was a night driver for Yellow Cab. My life will never be the same, and believe it or not, if I became a millionaire tomorrow—I'd still climb into my cab and drive a night or two every once in a while, because it is fascinating, addicting, rewarding, and because I am pretty good at it. Every call is a gamble, but unlike at the casino, the dealer pays you. I quickly found out that some very interesting things happen out there in the world that "normal" people rarely see, and I have written about some of them here.

This book, like most books, had lots of help being made, and I owe a debt of gratitude to many people. It had its beginnings when I would come home at dawn and tell Annie some of the events that had transpired the night before, as well as stories other drivers had told me when the night was quiet and we drifted together to pass the time. Annie told me that I should write them down, and I did. When I told her that some of the stories came to me in nearly poetic form, she encouraged me to explore that medium. I'm grateful she did. I guess that I should already have known this, but it took Annie to teach me that poetry was for everyone to write—something that I had not been taught in high school and college English and literature courses in the 1960s and '70s To her I owe a great debt of thanks, as this book wouldn't have been written without her encouragement. She also provided sound editorial council after the stories had been written, and was honest enough to tell me which ones simply didn't work at all. I followed her advice nearly completely, if only occasionally begrudgingly.

Our daughter Augusta also heard many of the stories and managed to provide encouragement despite the early hours and the fact that most often she was still in her pajamas. Augusta, Roland, Asa, and Johanna all provide inspiration in ways that would take a writer much better than I to put to words. They all have my deepest appreciation.

When the manuscript was approximately one-third finished, I passed it to a few friends at the University of New Mexico for comment. Ed De Santis, Garth Bawden, Lisa Huckell, Dave Stuart, and Marcel Harmon offered encouragement and asked to see more. Friends Mike and Beverly O'Brien said the same thing. With this support I brought that early portion of the manuscript to Luther Wilson, the director of UNM Press, and Beth Hadas, editor at the press and former director. Luther and Beth told me to finish it and bring it back.

I did, but there was at least one more stop along the way that the manuscript had to take. But it wasn't just any stop.

I had to give it to the drivers, dispatchers, and operators—my colleagues—to see what they thought of it. For a number of reasons, I was nervous. The world that I was describing was their world as well as mine, and I was nervous about my ability to capture it. In fact, to me it seemed almost pretentious to even attempt it. Despite my concerns, each and every person at Yellow Cab who read it was overwhelmingly supportive with kind words and constructive criticism. My major errors were in weaponry—certainly not my expertise—and thanks to the work of several colleagues I now stand corrected. Of course, cabdrivers never carry weapons, so please consider the parts where weapons are involved "fictionalized" by the author.

Now for the people from my Yellow Cab world who played a role in bringing this book to life. Phone operators Liz Early, Sharon Yeager, and Elaine Lopez offered many kind and supportive words. Sometimes, in the middle of the night, it seems that they might be the only sane voices out there in the world. Current and former dispatchers Jerry Merrill, Butch Cox, Chris Hazen, Bill Stryker, Doug Mueller, Ramona Baca, and Richie Panning (may he rest in peace) were not only supportive, they were also a constant source of inspiration. Cashiers Ruby Martin and Dave Register also deserve a word of thanks. Sitting behind the glass window all night long must give Dave lots of time to read and think—I have encountered few people with more fresh ideas than he about so many subjects. Dave's editorial advice on the manuscript is also appreciated.

In the front office of Yellow Cab, Patty Consterdine has always been a pleasure to work with, and I am grateful that she was always able to find a cab for me. I would also like to thank the owners of Yellow Cab, Steve Abraham and Billy G. Smith, for the opportunity to experience a world I never could have imagined.

Drivers and good friends Tom Cole, Mike Trujillo, Manny Clark, Dan Dempsey, and "D.J." Johnson read a nearly final draft and provided helpful feedback and encouragement. I am particularly grateful for the fact that Manny didn't beat the hell out of me after reading sections of the book.

Other drivers, former drivers, and friends who deserve a word of thanks are Mike Osmon, Ray Griego, Gordon Johnson, Dave Pinegar, Enrique Harrison, Troy Norris, Andrew Munz, Eduardo Castillo, Bernie Barlow, Julius A. Crockett, Saini Indjert, Victor Muniz, Bob Bradley, Harold Williams, Doug Larson, Russell Garrett, Neal Cleese, and Jerry Pierce.

Back at UNM Press, my thanks go to Luther Wilson, Beth Hadas, Maya Allen-Gallegos, Lincoln Bramwell, Lisa Pacheco, and Mina Yamashita for their help.

I would also like to thank my friend and former colleague Keith Basso, one of the finest writers I know, for his support and encouragement. Bruce Huckell and Jerry Green are always supportive, no matter the endeavor I undertake. I couldn't ask for better friends. My parents Robert and Marilynn Leonard taught me the values of reading, writing, and work. I hope it shows here. Family members Mary Ogle and Margaret Rhodes provided valuable comments and encouragement.

Finally, to all the anonymous fares out there in the world, thank you. Keep talking, and don't forget that big tips bring good karma.